perhaps tomorrow

 GALAXIE PRESS

perhaps tomorrow

TOM WIGGLESWORTH

For Jennifer

AUTHOR'S NOTE: This is a factual account of my experiences while in the custody of ZANU and Frelimo. However, for obvious reasons I am unable to confirm the veracity of statements made to me by members of those organisations whilst I was held by them.
T.W.

Published by Galaxie Press (Pvt) Ltd., P.O. Box 3041 Salisbury Zimbabwe

© Tom Wigglesworth
All rights reserved

Set 11/14 pt Century Schoolbook by Litho Services, Salisbury
Printed and bound by Mardon Printers, Bulawayo

ISBN 0 86925 116 3

He who forgives ends the quarrel

African proverb

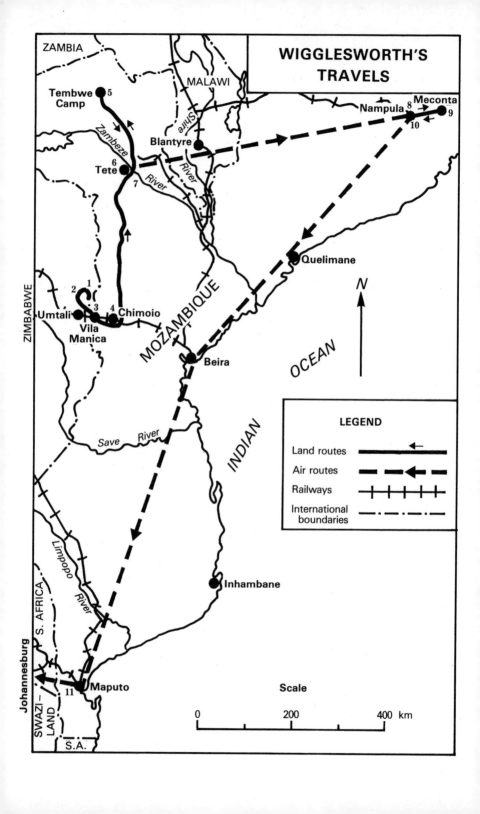

DATE	MAP REFERENCE	RECORD OF MOVES
1 August 1978	1	Captured at farm in Penhalonga.
1-4 August	2	Held in guerrilla camp in Rhodesia.
4-7 August	3	Marched to Vila Manica. Jailed there for two days.
7 August	4	Moved by landrover to Chimoio (Vila Pery) area. Kept in the bush outside Chimoio for about six weeks. Moved almost every day; long marches on foot.
10 September	5	Travelled by landrover to Tembwe area via Tete.
4 October	6	Transport by ambulance landrover to area about 30 kms south east of Tete and kept in the bush.
21 December	7	Handed over to Frelimo and kept in tent near Zambezi River.
27 December	8	Flown to Nampula by light aircraft.
27 December	9	By lorry to Meconta.
31 January 1979	10	Flown from Nampula to Maputo in large Russian-built aircraft.
2 February	11	In Maputo released into the care of Amnesty International.
4 February	12	Flown from Maputo to Jan Smuts airport (Johannesburg) on scheduled flight.

1

On the morning of Sunday 30 July 1978, jet aircraft from the south screamed above our house and turned, as usual, due east: another raid by the Rhodesian Air Force on guerrilla camps in the Chimoio area of Mozambique.

The morning of Tuesday 1 August 1978 dawned clear and fresh. There was in the typically crisp mountain air just a touch of frost and as usual the view from the bedroom window filled me with delight. Jennifer was out of bed before me at a quarter to six and busied herself in the kitchen getting the early morning tea. Since our arrival in Rhodesia we had never employed indoor servants for the experience of others had taught us that servants were often the willing or unwilling informers of guerrillas. We then listened to the six o'clock news together in the bedroom and after washing and dressing it was time for the early morning roll-call on the police radio network known as the Agric-Alert system. Outside the towns this system covered the country and enabled the most remote of farms and homesteads to be in constant touch with the nearest police headquarters.

Promptly at half past six my labour arrived for the day's orders and were given their tasks: Kenneth and Joseph were to clear a fallen tree near our circular drive and Ben was to work in the vegetable garden. At five minutes to seven Jennifer set off in the Datsun for the convoy start-point some three kilometres away. I went ahead in the Peugeot Station Wagon, keeping a sharp look out for disturbed earth in the dirt road which would indicate the possibility that mines had been laid during the previous night. With me in the Peugeot were the three dogs, Anna, Olga and Mitzi. I had also an automatic shotgun and a small FN automatic was concealed on my person. The convoy start-point was on the tarred road outside Jim Valintine's house: there the armed escort vehicle, manned by police reservists, was waiting. After the departure of the convoy I had a brief conversation with Jim Valintine, who informed me that there had been an attack on a homestead in the Old Umtali area the previous night. Old Umtali being on a different radio network, I had not been aware of this attack.

Returning to the farm I thought I would check on the two labourers dealing with the fallen tree and so I drove into the lower end of the drive and after stopping the car walked the few yards to where they should have been working. There was no sign of them. I returned to the car to let out my dogs, collected the shotgun and went to look for the men. I walked away from the house towards the lake and as the dogs dashed past me I looked up to see a lone figure dressed in green, wearing a pack and carrying an AK 47, moving through the trees in sunken ground between the lake and the dirt road which formed the boundary of my property with that of Jim Valintine.

I kept losing sight of him in the trees but glimpsed him as he crossed the dirt road. I was in the open on the fire break and when I reached the dirt road I had lost sight of him again. He had disappeared into the trees whilst I was standing on the dirt road, feeling very exposed. I then thought that I was being led into an ambush and decided to return to the house and report the incident on the Agric-Alert. I walked quickly back to my car returning the shotgun to its "travelling" position between the front seats. Closing the rear door of the car I realised that the dogs were no longer with me. For the first time I had the feeling that the situation may not be as I had supposed. It struck me that the lone guerrilla may originally have been moving towards the house and that my appearance on the scene had caused him to change direction.

Getting into the car to return to the house I made up my mind that I would keep alert. If I saw any further indication of the presence of terrorists I would accelerate past the house and return to Jim Valintine to use his Agric-Alert. I drove slowly the two or three hundred metres to the house but saw nothing suspicious and decided to park in my usual place outside the garage at the back of the dwelling. In this decision I was swayed by the fact that Jennifer and I had a long-standing arrangement that she would telephone me at ten minutes to eight each morning to report her safe arrival in Umtali.

As I got out of the car I heard the telephone ringing in the house. Of course the call may not have been for me as we were on a party line but nevertheless I left the car in a rush, leaving my shotgun between the seats. Feeling for the house keys I was mid-way between the car and the back stoep when a single shot was fired. I looked up and saw six armed guerrillas coming round the corner of the house to my right. I heard movement to my left and four guerrillas stood up from behind the sandbags on the stoep. A further four emerged from the garage. In the moment of almost palpable silence which followed the initial confrontation, my feelings moved between fear and indignation. Incongruously I registered that the telephone had stopped ringing and that the guerrillas were not dressed in any distinctive uniform, though green clothing predominated. I also mentally noted that

11

they were all armed, some with AK 47s and others with semi-automatic rifles. A young guerrilla, very smartly dressed and wearing a bush ranger's hat, came up to me. Holding his gun in his right hand he gave me a blow across the face with his left forearm. I fell to the ground and dropped the house keys. He then removed my watch from my wrist and searched my pockets where he found a bunch of keys which fitted the locks of the sheds and workshops.

The guerrilla asked me in good English: "Where is your money? Come on—where is it?"
At the same time he made as if to kick me in the ribs.

I replied: "I have no money. I am a poor farmer."

He looked unconvinced and continued his search of my pockets in a perfunctory way. He said: "If you had got out of the car with your gun I would have shot you." The others were chattering to each other in Shona and my assailant was also joining in. In the haste he failed to feel the small automatic which was in its leather holster on a belt around my waist and covered by my green jersey. I was hauled to my feet and led off into a plantation of pine and wattle trees to the north of the house for a distance of about 400 metres. Here I was ordered to lie on my back with my hands clasped behind my head. One man stood over me with his bayonet a few inches from my left eye. Three others squatted near me and lit cigarettes but kept their weapons in their hands. At this point the 'commander', whom I had not noticed before, came up to me. He was lean, wore a long-skirted coat and had a pronounced limp.

He said: "We are not going to kill you. We want to talk to you. Do you know the Skipwiths?" He spoke quietly, but with menace in his voice. As he addressed me I tried to sit up but one of the guards pushed the muzzle of his rifle into my chest with some force and I fell back. The Skipwiths were an elderly couple who successfully grew fruit on their farm near the Honde Valley. Some months before this date guerrillas had entered their property, mixing with the labour force as they started work in the early morning at about six a.m. They had questioned the Skipwiths, treating them roughly in the process, robbed the dwelling and then let them go. The couple had vacated their farm immediately after the guerrillas had left and had moved into Umtali.

"Yes", I replied, "I know them".

He then said: "We talked to them and let them go." I was encouraged by this. He went on: "Your workers speak well of you and your wife and asked us not to kill you. Kenneth has told us that you rescued his family from behind the wire. That is good." (This apparently referred to the time when Kenneth's family were to be moved into a 'protected village' and I had taken them into my farm compound to join their father). He then walked away towards the house with the other guerrillas except for four left behind as guards. From my position I could not see the house.

Some time later they returned festooned with clothing and goods looted from the house including all my suits, Jennifer's electric sewing machine, two transistor radios, a typewriter and lots of other things. Their pockets were bulging with loot and in addition they had used blankets as stretchers to carry food, drink and smaller items. I remember thinking that if they met the Security Forces they would have to drop the lot before they could fight or run away.

The leader spoke to my guards in Shona and then said to me: "Come on. Move! Move!"

I said: "What about our talk? May we have it now?"

He shouted forcefully: "Move! Move!" and pushed me in the direction we were to travel.

13

We formed up in single file, fifteen of us, but I suspected that there were others on the flanks, and we moved off in a northerly direction through Dane Farm. This farm was owned by Gordon Bradley who long ago had moved with his family into Umtali but kept a small staff of labourers at the farm.The guerrillas moved along as if the property belonged to them. Because of the loads they were carrying our pace was quite slow and no attempt was made to use cover. I was wearing a new pair of veldskoens and the patterned soles were leaving a well marked pattern in the dust. One of the guerrillas behind me came up and told me to take my boots off. I objected to this and while we were arguing the matter the column became split. The commander came back and after some discussion with the guerrilla told me to leave the track and walk in the long dry grass at the side. However, I kept my boots on. After a further three or four kilometres we stopped under some trees on a knoll and had a late picnic breakfast taken from my larder. They were so casual and carefree that my morale was at a low ebb, for they behaved as if they had already taken over the country. By this time both my radios were blaring out Shona dance music and the guerrillas were singing and shuffling to it. Whilst we were eating the commander told me to change my shorts for a pair of my long trousers carried by one of the guerrillas. This was most worrying for if I did so I could not fail to expose the automatic strapped round my waist. I decided to take a chance and put the trousers on over my shorts, at the same time tucking my green jersey, which covered the small gun and holster, into the top of the trousers. No objections were raised but already I could foresee that the little gun was going to prove an acute embarrassment. And so it was.

About this time one of the guerrillas approached me

14

holding the telephone in his hand. The telephone was on a plug so that it could be moved from room to room. I could not think why they had bothered to steal and carry it. However, this joker had a sense of humour for he enquired: "Would you like to ring the police? Perhaps you would like to telephone your wife?" At the same time he operated the dial. I ignored him. Throughout this march he constantly enquired if I wished to telephone anyone. I saw no attempts made to bury the empty beer bottles or food tins but this could have been done after I moved on.

After some time we turned west and eventually came up to the dirt road from Odzani to Watsomba. As we approached this road a cry of "motor" went up and a cloud of dust to our right confirmed that a large motor vehicle was approaching from the direction of Watsomba. At this time we were only about a hundred metres from the road, but in long dry grass. I was pulled down but not before I recognised an R.M.S. lorry travelling fast towards Odzani. How the driver failed to see us before we dropped into the grass I shall never know. After the departure of the lorry we resumed our march as casually as before and crossed the road like a school crocodile with the radios still playing. We now had a stiff climb in front of us without any cover except rocks, and the pace quickened. After some time I became visibly distressed and as soon as suitable cover was available the commander called a halt for a rest and the adjustment of loads. It was here that I heard the typewriter drop with a clatter. About ten minutes later we were on the move again and shortly we reached the top of the climb and turned left along the top of the ridge until we came to a large valley containing many huts. This valley appeared to be in the centre of three high ridges which formed a triangle. As the crow flies it could not have been more than eight to ten kilometres from my home. Now I was sure that I would not be released.

I was taken into a hut and given a chair. This hut was unusual in that it was divided into rooms and I could see beds and other furniture in the other rooms. Also there were many suitcases and boxes in sight, no doubt full of looted items. As soon as I arrived I was offered water and naartjies. These, already prepared for the market, had been taken from my fruit packing shed. In the next hour or so many men, women and children came to view the captured 'boss' and I felt like the first panda at the zoo. About four p.m. (judging by the sunlight) three girls came into the hut and stood in line in front of me giggling and nudging each other. Two of them were the usual well-fleshed African girls but the one in the centre was tall and slim and much better dressed than the others. After some minutes one of the guards in the hut walked up and stood at my side. He pointed to the girls and then he said to me: "You must select a camp wife."

I thought my ears must be deceiving me so I asked him to repeat what he had said.

He said again: "You must have a camp wife." A wife! I had heard of traditional Shona hospitality but this was five-star treatment with vengeance. I replied gravely: "I already have a wife. I don't need another one." None of the girls appeared to be disappointed by my rejection of the offer. In fact they continued giggling.

Then the tall girl in the middle made a sort of curtsey and said in good English: "My name is Samantha. I am 22 years of age and I am yours if you want me."

I was rather wary for I thought that this was an attempt to soften me up and thereby make me more cooperative. Later I was to learn that I had got rather the wrong end of the stick. "Thank you. I am honoured by your offer," I replied, "but I have no need of a wife." The girls just giggled again and nudged each other. Then they turned and left. The guards said nothing to me but they were obviously very amused by the whole affair.

I relapsed into thought and wondered what action Jennifer had taken after getting no reply from me on the telephone. Would she think that it was out of order? It often was in that hilly, forested country particularly now that so many estates were not maintained due to the absence of the owners. Would she ask the Penhalonga police to call me on the Agric-Alert? This would be inconclusive as I was seldom within reach of the set during the day. She would probably wait until lunch time before raising the alarm, knowing that if the telephone was out of order I would have made some effort to get in touch with her during the morning. I was full of concern for her. *I* knew what was happening whereas *she* would fear the worst. Poor Jennifer. Our idyllic life was at an end, it seemed.

After we had purchased the farm we had both worked very hard. Jennifer had had to take a job in Umtali until we could get the farm viable and I had employed the minimum of labour. We had to keep our costs down for we were unable to bring any further funds into the country; but always we'd hoped that commonsense would prevail and that there would be a political settlement. We could then transfer money from the U.K. and South Africa and really develop the property. We were very happy, though, and had no regrets. The surrounding countryside was full of natural beauty spots and each weekend we would pack a picnic lunch, take the dogs and walk for hours. This only lasted until the Mozambique border was closed in 1976 and Western Mozambique became a base for the ZANLA guerrillas.

With this the area became sinister and dangerous with ambushes and mined roads. A curfew was imposed between dusk and dawn which restricted travel after dark. Convoys had become the order of the day and when we went to Pretoria for a short holiday we had had to take four different convoys, necessitating overnight stops in hotels en route. The only entertaining done now was to visit neighbours for Sunday lunch. Walking any distance away from one's dwelling was foolish. There were numerous attacks on houses and persons in the area and more and more properties were vacated as the owners left for South Africa or sought sanctuary in Umtali or Salisbury.

Although we rejected the idea of a security fence we did have security lights fitted and prepared a helipad for helicopter landings. In addition I built sandbag walls outside each external door and sandbagged our bedroom window. All this was for assistance in repelling a night attack on the homestead which was the usual form of attack. Also all windows were fitted with external anti-grenade screens. For some time we had been on the Agric-Alert police warning radio network. We sometimes had visits from police reservist patrols but seldom if ever saw any soldiers. We fully realised that Rhodesia had insufficient manpower to be strong everywhere and the topography favoured the guerrillas. However, it often seemed that it was a case of closing the stable door after the horse had bolted and as is not unusual in these circumstances we sometimes thought there were far too many men in uniform wandering around the towns. We thought they would have been better employed on the isolated farms protecting the farmers and labour from attack and intimidation.

By 1978 our estate was in very good shape and I had planned double crops. However, the guerrilla threat was looming larger and I was particularly worried about Jennifer having to use the dangerous road beteen Umtali and Odzani twice a day at regular times. A convoy had been organised but there was only one escort vehicle and better protected convoys were constantly being attacked. We discussed the possibility of moving into Umtali and visiting the farm once a week but never decided anything. The truth was that we so loved the place that we did not want to leave. Vacated farmsteads had been vandalised. Doors, windows and even roofs had been stripped off.

We kept putting off making a decision—for which I was to blame, for Jennifer would always fall in with my plans. I would suggest we move after the broccoli was marketed; and then it would be after the fruit season. At the same time we had promised to look after the Strouds' property and their labour when they went on holiday to South Africa for a month. Whilst we had been away for a fortnight some time earlier our house had been entered and robbed twice. We had lost all our clothing, bedding and radios, and other effects including polo trophies and irreplaceable items collected from many countries in which I had served during my army and air force career. The official report from the police was that the robberies were the work of a civilian gang operating in the rural areas and not of terrorists. However, it was becoming obvious that law and order was fast breaking down and I should have said then that "enough is enough" and left the area.

At this time of the year, June-July, our main task was the clearing of fire breaks. This was a time and labour consuming operation which had to be carried out each year to counter the many veld fires which were usually started by carelessness or saboteurs. I had made a fire break completely round the boundary of my property and an inner circular fire break to protect the house and buildings. Also I did a lot of protective 'burning off' to supplement the fire break. In my case all this had to be done by hand as I had no tractors or ploughs and in addition to using my regular labour I had to employ women to do the outer fire break with *badzas*. It was essential to have this task completed before the high winds came in August and September. This took nearly a month of unproductive work. Meanwhile the other work had been accumulating . . . .

Just after last light I was ordered outside and again a single file was formed led by the man who had been in command during the morning. We numbered about ten or twelve and I was in the middle. We walked down a stony gully almost due west and in front of me I could see a kraal on my left. The kraal huts were in good condition, but deserted. I thought: "This is where I am going to be killed." Inside one of these huts no one would hear anything and in any case they would not use a gun but probably the bayonet. I felt rather desperate and determined to try and get the automatic from its hidden place, remembering Winston Churchill's war-time advice to "take one with you." The small gun was in a holster next to my skin on my left side under my shorts, jersey and trousers. I undid the zip of my trousers, pulled my jersey clear, undid the zip of my shorts and got the fingers of my right hand round the butt of the automatic. It was much more difficult to do this than it sounds, for all this time we were walking along a very rough and stony track. Imagine my dismay when I found that I could not move the gun; because of the day's exertion it was firmly jammed in the holster. This had happened before and so I had cut away the ring of leather at the muzzle end of the holster so that I could insert the middle finger of my left hand to push the gun up into my right hand.

As I was attempting this the guerrilla some five paces behind me spoke to me in Shona. I withdrew my hands. He closed up to me and said in English: "What you doing?" I turned round to face him and showed him my empty hands. I then pointed to my open zip and said I was closing the zip of my trousers. He grunted but remained close to my heels. By this time I was relieved to find that we had passed the kraal. I was not to be killed there.

We were still descending into the valley and when we reached the bottom we halted. All round us was a rocky outcrop and in front a steep rocky climb to the ridge. The commander gave a series of low whistles and presently from out of the dark emerged five figures all carrying AK 47s. They talked among themselves for a minute or two and then the newcomers came to talk to me. Two of them spoke passable English and asked me questions as to where I came from and what I did and so on. These questions were repeated hundreds of times over the next few months as every guerrilla of whatever rank was entitled, it seemed, to talk to me and ask questions.

After about fifteen minutes, accompanied by the newcomers, we made our way back to the camp. Here we all entered a larger hut filled with smoke from a wood fire burning in the centre. There were no rooms or partitions. I was told to sit down on the earth floor with my back to the wall. Two guards were placed one on each side of the door on the opposite side of the hut to me and the others sat on their haunches round the fire. Presently a bowl of water and supply of *sadza* were brought in. They came to me with the water so that I might wash my right hand before eating the *sadza* but I refused the food. I did not like it but tried hard to eat it later on when it was the only food available.

Now, I thought, this is the opportunity to get the automatic into the pocket of my jacket. The guards at the door were obscured by the smoke and the other guerrillas were busy round the fire eating their *sadza* and talking, talking, talking. There were no lights in the hut. I went through the unzipping routine and struggled to get my left hand under the muzzle to ease the automatic from the holster. I appeared to be succeeding when there was a loud cry in Shona from a child's voice. A small boy of about ten years whom I had not noticed had been watching me, curiously observing my unusual activity. At his cry there was a rush towards me and I was smothered by bodies, hitting and kicking me and tearing off my clothes. I was left lying naked on the floor with four guards standing over me whilst the remainder returned to the fire with my clothes and gun. If I attempted to move I was threatened. Meanwhile a noisy argument appeared to have broken out round the fire and both Shona and English were being shouted. It seemed to me that my immediate fate was being discussed and I thought that there would be only one answer.

After some time had elapsed the commander who had captured me came and said: "You should be killed. You tried to shoot us."

I made no reply.

He continued after a long pause: "I have decided that you will not be killed, yet. You must go to Chimoio to be questioned. I am sure you are a soldier, a leader."

I said: "I am no longer a soldier. I am a farmer."

He grunted in reply. He then said: "You will be in handcuffs from now on." He then walked back to the fire.

Later some of my clothes were returned to me supplemented with some of theirs. Presumably some clothing had been destroyed or damaged in the struggle for the gun. While dressing I discovered that during the struggle I had suffered no broken bones but I was badly bruised all over my body and legs. My head and face had not been hit but I had a broken tooth and a swollen eye from the blow during my capture in the morning. I felt no resentment for the beating but only relief that I was not to be killed. Not yet, anyway. My military experience had taught me that all frightened men get cruel and angry and most soldiers would have behaved in like manner when they realised that a supposedly helpless unarmed prisoner still had a concealed gun. I could recall German prisoners during the Second World War being roughly handled when they were searched and a hidden knife or bayonet was discovered.

After I had dressed the handcuffs were put on and I was taken outside by four guards. We walked to the top of a ridge preceded by a girl carrying blankets. When we reached the ridge I noticed that there were many men sleeping on the ground. One of the guards told me in English to lie on the blanket. He then bound my ankles together with rope and a second blanket was placed on top of me. The four guards, who also had two blankets each, then placed themselves around me one on either side, and one at my feet and one at my head. The English-speaking guard seemed to be in charge and lay down to my right only a couple of metres away. That night was long and miserable. I was stiff and sore all over and the handcuffs were too tight. Because of the slope I kept slipping off the blanket and I gradually moved downhill until my feet touched the guard lower down. The top blanket rolled up under my arms. Being bound hand and foot I could do nothing to improve my situation and it was bitterly cold with heavy frost. I thought that this must be some new form of torture. To offer me a young 'wife' and then to bind me hand and foot! Perhaps if I had not foolishly kept the automatic I might not have had the handcuffs and rope round my ankles. I might have been able to slip away. 'If only' and 'perhaps' were always in my thoughts; but there was no future in thinking like that. I must have dozed off just before dawn.

I was awakened by movement all round me. There were fifty or more guerrillas on the hillside all getting up and folding their blankets. The girls from the huts were already climbing the hill to collect the blankets. The removal of my handcuffs was a painful operation as my wrists were very swollen. I always hated this time during the next four days. The four guards and I made our way down the steep hill. I moved very painfully and slowly. Then I was taken into a different hut from the two I had occupied the previous day. Here I met a guerrilla who informed me that he was the one I had chased before my capture the previous morning. In the hut were his wife and his young son. They were having *sadza* and tea. They offered me some. I drank the tea which was too sweet for my taste but very, very welcome.

Later that morning I was taken into yet another hut and had fresh guards. Throughout my imprisonment this changing of the guards was always very upsetting. One quickly got to recognise the guards who showed some compassion and sympathy; some guards developed a liking for me. When they changed, all was suspicion and hostility again until everyone thawed out a little.

That afternoon I had an extremely unpleasant experience whilst in the care of the guerrilla who had struck me across the face the previous morning. It was the same man who had searched me and taken the watch and keys. He was young, about eighteen years, very smartly dressed and good looking with regular features and beautiful teeth. Apparently he had been reprimanded (or perhaps worse) for failing to find the automatic when he had searched me. Anyway that afternoon he was one of my guard of four. He sent two of the guards outside the hut to sit on a bank and watch the door from outside. The remaining guard he sent off on an errand. This left me alone in the hut with him and his AK 47. I was sitting on a low chair half asleep when I received a lash across my face and neck from a long baggage strap which I had used on the roof rack of my car. I instinctively got up from the chair and made towards him. He dropped the strap and grabbed his gun and shouted at me to go back and sit down. At the same time he cocked his gun and pointed it at me. The two guards outside rushed to the door and spoke to my assailant in Shona. By this time I was back on the chair. The two guards were apparently satisfied with his explanation for they returned to their position on the bank out of sight. The face of the young guerrilla was contorted with hate and he was muttering to himself. He said: "I am going to beat you. You're stupid. Why did you hide that gun?" He shouted hysterically: "Why? Why? Why? You should have been killed!"

Again he picked up the leather strap. Fortunately for me, he had the buckle in his hand. He lashed at my head. However, I was now prepared and putting up my arms one on either side of my head I took the blows on my forearms. All the time this was going on he kept saying in a low voice: "You are stupid! What are you? You are stupid." In my predicament I was inclined to agree with him!

He kept this up for about fifteen minutes (although it seemed longer) until the fourth guard was heard approaching. The following afternoon there was a repeat performance although this time he had arranged for an audience of girls and older women. I was gratified to see the look of disgust on the faces of the older women and the young ones soon got bored and went away. I later was to learn that if I had reported his sadistic behaviour he would have been severely beaten. The ZANLA forces claim to have a code of conduct towards prisoners based on the *Thoughts of Mao Tse Tung* and all are taught this code.

I continued to spend the nights on the mountain side, handcuffed and with my ankles bound; but I did persuade them to select a level piece of ground. At night I always had the same four guards and one night the English-speaking one introduced me to the girl carrying the blankets and said that she was his wife. She got into his blankets with him and twice during the night I was disturbed by his exertions and heavy breathing and by her low moaning. Just before dawn she returned to her hut.

One morning what I had feared came to pass. The guerrilla with the key to my handcuffs had been called away during the night and had taken the key with him. I complained continuously the next morning and just after midday he arrived full of apologies and said he had forgotten about them. By this time my wrists were painfully swollen and the following night he put them on much more loosely.

I had been captured on the Tuesday morning and had eaten very little since, living on my fat as it were. I had been offered food, mostly *sadza*, but was not attracted enough to make the effort to eat it.

On the evening of Thursday I was taken to a large hut with the usual wood fire in the centre. One of my worst discomforts was the heavy smoke in the huts and many times I thought I was going to faint. I never understood how some of the girls could spend the whole day and night in these smoke-filled huts without any outward sign of ill effects. In the hut to which I was taken was the commander who had captured me. He told two of the guards to stay outside the door whilst two were allowed inside the hut. There were no other occupants.

Before unlocking and removing my handcuffs he said: "You see that door. If you go through that door without me you will be killed." He walked to the far side of the hut and returned with an enamel mug and offered it to me. I hesitated about drinking the contents. He laughed and fetched a wine bottle. I recognised it as the same as some I had brought back from South Africa some weeks before. He said: "It is from your house." I said nothing but sipped the wine and recognised that it was a Grünberger Stein.

When I entered the hut he had been playing Shona dance music on a battery-operated, portable record player. There were only five seven-inch records and he continued to play them over and over again whilst I was there. The volume was at full pitch but realising I could not hear what he was saying he turned it down.

He said: "I told you I would talk to you and let you go but you lied to me. After searching your house I found evidence that you are helping the Security Forces. You are a mercenary leader."

I replied: "That is not so. I have nothing to do with the Security Forces or mercenaries. I am over sixty and too old for military service. I am growing fruit and vegetables for the Umtali market."

He said: "You are lying. You had two police radios, many guns and lots of ammunition. You have medals and there are pictures of you in uniform." (Here he produced some photographs of me in uniform which had been kept in an old brief-case together with the medals and other military service documents.)

I then replied: "The police radio and some of the guns and ammunition are not mine but belong to a friend. I am looking after them for him whilst he is in South Africa".

He replied: "I do not believe you. You are lying. Why did you not help us? Many white farmers are helping us."

I looked at him with an expression of disbelief on my face. He continued. "You do not believe me. Do you know . . . (here he mentioned the names of five whites living in the area of Odzani and Honde Valley). They are all helping us with food and do not report us. They will not be attacked."

I did not believe him at that time. I thought that he was trying to obtain my co-operation by suggesting that I was the odd man out! He said: "There are hundreds of whites all over the country helping us in the struggle but not you. You are a soldier."

I replied: "I am retired and no longer a soldier."

"Retired? What is retired?" I tried to explain but he cut me short. He continued: "You know you should have been killed when you drew that gun. My comrades wanted to kill you. I stopped them because you must go to Chimoio for questions by the High Command. What have you got to say?"

"I have nothing to do with the Security Forces," I replied. "Surely you can find that out without my having to go to Mozambique." There was a pause here and I said: "I am hungry and cannot eat *sadza*."

He replied: "You will have to eat *sadza*. There is nothing else. It's good food and the comrades have only *sadza* and sometimes vegetables. They can walk all day and night on this food." After attending to the record player he returned and said: "You should have gone to Chimoio tonight but a comrade has not arrived. It is now too late as it is a long way and must be done in the dark."

I then said: "When I came here I was offered a girl wife but then you put handcuffs on me and bound my ankles. Is that some form of Chinese torture?"

He looked as if he did not understand this and I attempted to explain my meaning.

Suddenly he clapped his hands together and roared with laughter. He spoke in Shona to the guards who were one on either side of me. They did not seem to get the point either but after some crosstalk they laughed loud and long and slapped hands with each other. The commander still laughing turned to me and at great length and with much repetition explained that the girls were in the camp to wait on the guerrillas as orderlies, to do the cooking and as and when possible to cross into Mozambique for training as nurses and political commissars. If unsuitable for this they did the laundry and cooking at the main camp in Mozambique. They were all volunteers and none was held against her will. Some of the women and children in the camp were the families of the comrades who had run away from the Security Forces. The three girls I had seen had all volunteered to act as my orderly whilst I was in that camp. All the comrades there had an orderly. (I had always observed that all the guerrillas had a particular girl waiting on them, fetching their food and lighting their cigarettes and I had assumed that they were girl friends or wives. Often the girls approached the men on their knees). Some of the girls were used as couriers and visited the towns regularly as contacts gathering information.

I was also told that in ZANLA no sex was permitted between comrades outside marriage. This was on the orders of the President of ZANU, Robert Mugabe. I learnt later that this order was not popular with everyone and in the nature of things was not always obeyed. If an unmarried girl became pregnant she went away to a refugee camp to have the child and stayed with the child until it was weaned. She then returned to her duties leaving the child with an 'adopted mother' or relative. I never found out what happened to the father of the child if he was known.

I commented to the commander that I had been amazed at the noisy and leisurely way we had walked to the camp. Did they not fear a follow-up from the Rhodesian Security Forces?

He replied: "I would know well in advance if there were Security Forces in the area for the masses are on the side of the guerrillas." He added: "There has been no military follow-up in this area for months although sometimes police visit the scene of an incident." He admitted that he avoided contact with the Security Forces because "that is guerrilla warfare." His greatest concern was with spotter aircraft and helicopters (I had noticed already that when spotter aircraft and helicopters flew over the men rushed into the huts whilst the women and children pottered about outside).

He continued: "The ridges are manned night and day and only an air attack could dislodge or destroy us." (Later, after my release, I was informed that the camp had been bombed the day after I had left for Mozambique).

The guerrilla commander asked: "Can you walk fast?"

I replied: "I can walk all day at *my* pace."

He laughed and said: "The comrades are fit and can walk very fast. They can walk 40 miles in one night." (I thought this an exaggeration but was later to learn that it was near the truth.)

He then said: "You will find the walk to Mozambique very hard and you had better start eating *sadza.*"

He spoke to the guards in Shona and the handcuffs were put on. The guards pushed me towards the door with the guerrilla commander in front of me. He spoke to the guards outside the hut and then returned to the record player and increased the volume. I was taken into another smoke-filled hut already crammed with girls and guerrillas.

After some time I was escorted on to the mountain ridge preceded by a girl carrying blankets. For this rough, steep climb I was handcuffed to a guerrilla and progress in the dark was slow and painful. Another long cold night with wrists and ankles secured; but much to think about. I was particularly concerned with the names of the 'white helpers' given to me earlier that evening. Some of them were very vociferous supporters of Smith and the Rhodesian Front party. It couldn't be true—or could it? Anyway I decided then and there that I would never divulge those names. It would be most unfair.

The following morning I was taken to yet another hut with the usual fire and smoke. By now I had grown bold enough to stand by the customary hole in the wall which served as a window. The guards did not mind, providing I kept still and did not attempt to walk about, but if they heard an aircraft they pulled me down to the floor. One of the girls brought in a pillow slip which was oozing yellow liquid at the bottom and she showed me the contents which appeared to be many eggs most of which were smashed. One of the girls told me that they had come from my larder and asked if I would like some. I told them that I loved scrambled eggs. Eventually I was handed a plate covered with the eggs, fried and with lots of eggshell mixed in it. However, I enjoyed this, my first meal for days. With the eggs I had sweet biscuits!

Later that morning the tall girl who had offered to be my 'camp wife' or rather, my orderly, came into my hut. She began to rummage in an old suitcase. She pulled out some clothing and was on her way out when she stopped and said: "I am now going on a mission to Umtali."

This was an opportunity I could not miss. "Please, would you take a message to my wife to tell her that I am alive and well. My wife works at Halsteds—do you know where that is?"

The girl stopped. She looked as though she would help me. "Yes, I know where Halsteads is ... And I know about your wife." She thought for a moment. "No. I cannot take any messages. It is not allowed," she said emphatically.

"Couldn't you give it to someone else to give to her?" I pleaded. "No, I cannot. But good luck. You will not be here when I return."

Once again I indulged in 'if only' thoughts. Perhaps if she had been my 'orderly' I might have got her to change her mind. I doubt it as they all seemed very 'security conscious' and very loyal to their leaders.

The remainder of the day passed very slowly and I tried to sleep for I had a strong suspicion that I had a long walk ahead of me; but the smoke and noise in the hut defeated me. I thought over my capture and the three days following and wondered if I could have escaped or made a fair attempt. I also remembered my training in the British Army where I had learnt that if one is taken prisoner the best time to escape is as soon as possible after capture before the security is organised and you are in a strange country. To start with I had believed the 'commander' when he said that he wanted to talk with me and then let me go. Obviously that had been wishful thinking on my part and I had wanted to believe it. In addition, although I doubted if they would have advertised their whereabouts by firing long bursts at me, they were always close at hand and in large numbers and certainly fitter and more fleet of foot than I was. Darkness would have provided the best opportunity but I had been handcuffed and bound from the first night. I would have to wait for an opportunity on my way to Mozambique for I thought there would be little chance after I reached the guerrilla headquarters in that country.

Long before sunset I sensed that something was afoot. There was a certain amount of preparation of kit going on and the meal was served earlier. Sometimes during the afternoon two or three of the guerrillas paraded before me like mannequins wearing my suits, hats and overcoat. One character angered me by wearing my medals and miniatures and with one of my pipes in his mouth. The medals were pinned just to the left of his navel! I asked for the medals and pipe to be returned to me but there was only loud laughter in reply. However, later that night the pipe was given to me. I had no tobacco. On a previous day I had seen children playing with the coins from my treasured coin collection. I had also been informed with some malicious glee that out expensive sewing machine, Jennifer's pride and joy, had been buried in the ground. After laboriously carrying it to their hideout they had discovered it was an electric machine!

A further irreplacable loss was a box of catalogued camera slides recording our visits to various countries. Some of these were shown to me for identification and then handed round to the guerrillas in the hut. It was all very depressing.

2

Just before last light I was taken outside, closely guarded, and the column began to form up for the long walk. There appeared to be about twenty men and about ten girls. Before moving off they all sang a freedom-fighting song in which the word Zimbabwe frequently occurred. Once again I was amazed at the boldness of their attitude; no sneaking out after dark with the minimum of noise. During our conversation the previous night the 'commander' had mentioned that the curfew was in their favour; and so it appeared. Immediately after the singing we moved off and I was astounded to see that we were heading due west, the opposite direction from the border. From then on I never really knew where we were.

The night was very dark and I discovered to my dismay that I appeared to suffer from night blindness (for the past two or three years I had not been out of the house after dark because of the curfew which had completely curtailed social calls). Once again we were following rocky gullies downhill and before long I was slipping and falling every few steps. The pace was very fast and even the guerrillas were finding the going far from easy. They were carrying their weapons and ammunition and in addition seemed to be wearing many suits coats and mackintoshes. Some had heavy packs, no doubt full of looted goods, documents and the like. In Rhodesia we had known for a long time that some dead guerrillas were found wearing as many as three suits and three or four watches. In addition they wore many gold rings, bracelets and necklaces. They did this because they never knew if they would return to the base they had left. I soon found the going very trying and although there was a cold wind blowing I was soaked in perspiration. I will never forget that night and many times I wished for death to overtake me. Often I fell and was roughly hauled to my feet. My left foot and leg were almost beyond use for I had a twisted ankle, a swollen knee, and at some stage in the night a machine gun was dropped on my left foot damaging two toes rather severely. After one short halt I sank to the ground and could not sit up again. I was told that if I did not get up and get moving I would be shot. I told them to go ahead for that would suit me fine. However, they pulled me to my feet and one guerrilla was told to put his rifle across my back and push me whilst the one in front of me grabbed me by the wrist and pulled. The trouble was that the pace was altogether too fast for me and I had to run to keep up. Come to think of it, I must have been a damn nuisance to them as they were in a desperate hurry to cross the border into Mozambique before first light.

Some time during the night we stopped at a large kraal to pick up recruits for training in Mozambique and here we appeared to change commanders. While this was being organised with the usual incessant chattering in Shona I was taken into each of the huts in turn to be shown off. Each hut was crammed with old men, women and children. Some of the men cursed me and some of the women spat at me. I was beyond caring about my reception and was only glad of the rest from the 'jogging'. After I had got a second (or third) wind the guards in front and behind were relieved of their pulling and pushing duty. However, I was soon in trouble again for as we moved across the veld I lost contact with the man in front of me and in the absence of anything like a path did not know in which direction to go. I stopped and so perforce did all those behind me. There was much cursing and pushing but those behind me were no wiser as to the way to take. One of the commanders ran in front of me whistling to try and establish contact with the front half of the column, and two guerrillas returned to show the way. I received kicks and punches for my carelessness but at the first opportunity I pointed out that the man in front of me was wearing dark clothing which I could not see beyond five metres whilst the one behind me had one of my white raincoats draped over his shoulders which could be seen for quite a distance. I suggested that they should change places. This was done but at the same time I was told roughly to keep close up to the man in front. I am sure that the guerrilla with my raincoat was pleased to go in front of me for he must have been fed up with pulling me to my feet every time I slipped and fell. And so the night wore on. Both my legs were now badly bruised from the falls and collisions with rocky projections which I had been unable to avoid. The night remained dark. I became aware that we were travelling due east when, breasting a hill, I could see the lights of Umtali about four miles away on my right hand side. We were now in well forested country and, walking through trees, the going became easier. This was probably the Imbezi Valley.

Just before dawn we paused and one of the guerrillas whispered that we were now in Mozambique. I had not observed any signs of a minefield or border. This surprised me. Living in Odzani we had heard much of the 'cordon sanitaire' between us and the Mozambique border. Thousands of land-mines had been laid from Umtali to the north to prevent or hamper the crossing of guerrillas from Mozambique. From my home I had often heard the mines exploding, both by day and night, and wondered if it was guerrillas or animals that had caused the detonations.

We continued for about another hour and the girls at the back of the column over-took us and were sent on in front on their own. We moved off the track and lay down in the wet grass. After about half an hour, in daylight, we continued to walk. We seemed to have yet another fresh column commander, a young man dressed smartly in green. From his appearance he had not been on the strenuous walk of the night before: the other guerrillas appeared dirty and exhausted. Some were limping as badly as I was.

From now on the march had a relaxed, holiday air about it. Apart from four guards who stuck closely to me the whole time, the column split up into small groups who constantly overtook each other in a sort of walking competition. For myself I could just walk mechanically and any extra movement was sheer agony. We still had some steep climbing to do through pine trees which appeared to go right over a mountain top. Half way up I sank down against a tree to get my breath. Only the four guards were near me and in the relaxed atmosphere two of them had walked on when I sat down. I thought that here was my chance to back down the hill if the remaining two guards went in front of me. The undergrowth under the young pines was quite thick and there was lots of cover. However, the two guards also wanted a rest and sat down with their backs against trees only a few yards away from me holding their rifles at the ready. It was a forlorn hope as I was in no fit state to do any dashing about. I was determined to stay there as long as possible but after a few minutes I was ordered to get up and move on. Going down the other side of the mountain was a painful business and I practically wore out the seat of my trousers. The guards found it all rather amusing but they were not unkind. As I staggered along, where possible two walked one on either side of me whilst the other two followed behind. The man on my right had been a schoolteacher in Salisbury and was very keen to talk. Apart from relating his life history, ambitions and the reasons for his joining the guerrillas he told me that now I was in Mozambique all my worries were over. I would get good medical care for my feet and legs, good food and finish up in a nice house in Maputo. If I wished I could have my wife with me; if not I could go to England after two months. This was music to my ears and raised my morale no end. However, I had doubts as this guerrilla was of no rank as far as I knew—and what could he know of my future fate? (I was to learn later that they were always prepared to tell you what they thought you wanted to hear rather than the unpleasant truth. It was not lying, exactly, but was done to raise your morale. They were obsessed with morale-raising. It was indulged in by all ranks from the highest to the lowest. I sometimes made the mistake of thinking I was being promised something which subsequently did not materialise but I was wrong in this assumption. It was not meant like that at all.)

I had not seen a sign of the 'commander' since we had set off that morning but he was waiting for me at the bottom of the slope with three others. He shouted at my guards in Shona, apparently to the effect that we were a long way behind everybody else and they had better get a move on, or else. They explained that I could not or would not walk any faster. Whereupon the 'commander', a young dandy who had not walked a step the previous night, came up to me and started to shout at me in Shona, his face about a metre from my own. I just glared back at him, not understanding a word, but gathering that he was threatening me with a fate worse than death. Realising I did not speak Shona he changed to English and repeated his threats. Strengthened by the morale-boosting conversation with the ex-school teacher I told him that I was doing my best, that I could not move faster and suggested he organise a stretcher party to carry me. Thereupon I complacently put my empty pipe in my mouth and moved away to sit down. He lost his temper and grabbed at the pipe breaking yet another tooth. I must confess I hated him then and I told him that as soon as I reached his headquarters I would report him to a senior commander. This was a shot in the dark as at this time I was unaware that they had any sort of code of conduct towards prisoners. Anyway, the threat quietened him down and we set off again at my pace. Meanwhile he had my pipe in his mouth. A little later he came up to me and offered me a packet of cigarettes (made in Rhodesia I noted); I accepted thinking that I could strip them apart and use the tobacco in the pipe. However, he kept the pipe.

Before we had crossed the mountain that morning we had come across a deserted Mozambiquan homestead with citrus trees. There were some oranges on the trees but they were stale and the skins were hard and brittle. However, I filled my pockets with them and although it was impossible to eat them whilst walking I was glad of them later. There was nothing else to eat but I drank water at every opportunity.

We were now a party of eleven, the 'commander' with an AK 47, a crony of his without a weapon and eight guerrillas with AK 47s and SARs. After sending four of the guerrillas ahead the commander informed me that he was going to visit some Frelimo friends nearby who were celebrating a wedding that afternoon and that

I must go with him. I hoped that it was not too far off the beaten track but thought the rest might do me good. We left the dirt road and walked a short way cross-country until we reached a collection of huts at various levels on a steep slope. There were three or four huts at each level with steps up and down to each next level. The whole area was clean and tidy and apparently all the occupants of these many huts were inter-related. Preparations for the ceremony were in full swing and already much local beer had been consumed. None of the Mozambiquans spoke in English (in Mozambique the common language is Portuguese; only in Beira and Maputo is English heard to any extent and this is due to tourism but my guards acted as interpreters. Two of them including the 'commander', spoke Portuguese and English.

The village was crowded with family and guests including Frelimo soldiers in smart green uniforms. I was treated with courtesy and given a chair but one old character who turned out to be the bride's grandfather kept coming and shouting abuse and insults at me. I just laughed at him for he had obviously already celebrated well but not wisely. Whenever he was observed shouting at me he was quietly led away. I was continuously pressed to drink the home brew beer but with my stomach empty and much walking ahead of me I declined except for a mouthful to toast the bride. Fortunately I did not care for the taste of the beer. Some time later the father of the bride made me some tea (the water had not boiled) and gave me some homemade mealie cakes. By this time my guards had dispersed in the crowd and were obviously enjoying themselves. The 'commander' was the life and soul of the party and had an obvious liking for the local brew. I began to think that this might be my chance to walk back to Rhodesia. I would have to wait for an opportunity as I was the object of much interest from Frelimo soldiers in a group close by and if I started to wander about they would warn the guerrillas.

Eventually the bride and her two bridesmaids emerged from one of the huts and I was astounded at their appearance. I am no good at describing women's clothes and have often thought that women take great care in dressing to impress a man, or men, although most men, never notice what they wear. Perhaps women dress to impress other women. Anyway the bride and her maids would have been acceptable at a social wedding in Johannesburg or Durban and one can only wonder at the care and trouble that had been taken in this village in the bush. They shone like bright lights in this rather drab gathering. The actual ceremony took place at a dwelling on the lower level. I was on the top level and saw little of the event. However, there was a distinct thinning of the crowd around me and the Frelimo soldiers had moved off down the steps. It was now or never for a break. Unfortunately the obvious way out was down the steps where the ceremony was being held but that was where the guerrillas were. I would have to go back up the slope and hope that no one spotted me. I got up from the chair and began to move about getting some life into my legs. So far so good: nobody seemed bothered. I carefully looked up the slope to select a possible route. There were several paths from the three or four houses on the top level but the cover between the paths was only knee high. I decided to move slowly behind one of the houses to keep it house between me and the fiesta. Once I got behind the house I would pause and select my next route to the top of the slope. The pause would give me time to know if I had been spotted.

And now fate intervened in the shape of the drunken grandfather. I was about to wander round the blind side of the house when he came up to me shouting obvious obscenities and threatening to strike me. The old man was making a most awful din shouting and screaming and of course some people came to my 'rescue' including two of the guerrillas. That was that; for I was not left alone again. Shortly afterwards the 'commander' came along and we set off for Vila Manica. He then told me that the rest of the guerrillas would be waiting ahead of us because we were all to be picked up by Frelimo lorries at a certain point and taken to Vila Manica. I remarked that it was hardly worth the lorry ride as we must be close to Vila Manica with all this walking. However, my sarcasm was lost on him and he muttered that they must enter Vila Manica by Frelimo lorry for there was to be some sort of reception.

As we walked I noticed a dirt road on our right with the sign post 'To The Frontier'. So near and yet so far! After four or five kilometres we came across some of our party of the previous night sitting at the side of a tarred road. They said that the girls and some of the guerrillas had already gone by lorry to Vila Manica and they were waiting for the lorry to return. After about half an hour the lorry returned with four Frelimo soldiers in the back and one beside the driver. We all climbed on. But I managed only with some difficulty. We had to stand shoulder to shoulder as there was a large number of passengers. The lorry set off at breakneck speed and, to add to our discomfort, we were all showered with clouds of dust. The lorry seemed to have its nearside wheels off the road.

Now followed a 'ceremony' it will be difficult to describe. We halted outside a small police barracks. Opposite, on the other side of the road, was a small open space containing many trees and a number of park seats, most of them broken. I was given my usual escort and told to sit on a nearby park bench. The guerrillas were drawn up in two ranks with their backs to me on the same side of the road as I was. Opposite them were Frelimo police in front of the main entrance of the barracks. Close to the police commander was a large number of cardboard boxes. The guerrilla commander took up his position between the two parties and to a flank. He then proceeded to call out a series of names and one of the guerrillas would march over to where the police were standing. The commander of the police party would put his hand into one of the boxes and withdraw an article of clothing. It was a sort of lucky dip. Out came a jersey or a scarf or perhaps a balaclava. There was much saluting. The guerrilla commander had a peculiar salute which involved stamping both feet and moving his head down to meet his hand. Many times I thought he would fall over. I don't know why but I kept thinking of the Major-General from Gilbert and Sullivan. I did not think that the guerrillas were very impressed with their presents and I thought of all the suits, shirts, cardigans and jerseys they had taken from my house.

In the middle of the ceremony the guerrilla commander was called away by a man in civilian clothes who I later discovered was a police captain. He apparently was inquiring about my presence. During the absence of their commander and without further orders the tired guerrillas lay down on the grass verge behind them and went to sleep. Meanwhile a long, loud argument was going on between the police captain and the commander. This gave me a fresh hope. After all I had broken no laws in Mozambique and perhaps the police captain was insisting on my release. (What it is to be British and to think in terms of British laws and justice!) The whole discussion was in Portuguese. After some time the commander returned to his position in the middle of the road and after much shouting the guerrillas got painfully to their feet. The ceremony re-started. After the distribution of clothing both sides went through a series of saluting exercises and it was obvious that the guerrilla commander did not know how to say goodbye. His men were becoming weary of the whole thing. Eventually they were dismissed and it was now my turn.

It was obvious that I was going to be handed over to the Frelimo police and soon my guards were relieved by armed policemen. I had made up my mind to protest my innocence to the police captain and ask to be put in touch with the British counsul in Maputo. I was escorted across the road to the barracks and told to sit down in a small room containing four chairs, a table and a typewriter. After the arrival of the captain, with two others, the guards were told to wait outside the door. What followed was both frustrating and irritating. The captain spoke no English. His interpreter was a teenaged boy with a pleasant smile who spoke little English. The third man was a police clerk who was meant to type the questions and answers in Portuguese. He seemed to do very little typing for it was rather beyond him.

I started off by claiming that I had been illegally kidnapped and that I was a British citizen. I asked to be put in touch with the British Consul in Maputo. I also asked to have medical treatment for my damaged legs and feet. The interpreter was obviously not having much success with all this judging by the repetition and the puzzled look on the captain's face. Every so often he would hold up his hand to stop me in full flow in order to get some sense from the interpreter. I went on to claim that I could not be detained as I had not broken the law of Mozambique—unless they charged me with illegal entry. (This was meant to be a joke but it was quite wasted on them). Because of my leg and foot injuries, continued,

I would like to be accommodated in a hotel before proceeding to Maputo. I had no money but the British Consul would pay. All this took some time and was received most gravely by the captain. Here I started to remove my left boot and stocking but he was not having that and said that that was not necessary. I began to have hopes that I was having some success. A lot of conversation went on, in Portuguese, between the captain and the interpreter. The captain then informed me that I would have to spend that night in the police barracks for my own protection. He continued by saying that I must understand that white people were not popular in Mozambique and I could be attacked or killed by one of the 'masses'. This was a blow; and he ignored my reference to the British Consul. I then again pointed out that I could not be his prisoner as I had not offended against the laws of Mozambique. If he was going to detain me, on what charge was I being held? (This was a stupid question in Mozambique at that time and he ignored it). I then asked him if I could have a bed and mattress and again started to unlace my boot. Once again he stopped me with a wave of his hand and eventually it was agreed that attempts would be made to get me a bed and mattress. After a few more laboured questions and answers he got up and went out. I glanced at the paper in the typewriter and noticed that the sheet was almost clear. Perhaps they were going to type it all from memory. I wished them joy for certainly I was confused with the interview. The guards at the door were called in and I was led to a cell at the front of the building.

The cell was long and narrow with a barred window at the front of the building. This window was set at normal window height which was unusual for a cell. Attempts had been made to cover the window with cardboard but this had been torn in many places along the bottom to provide 'peep holes'. I was to learn very quickly that looking into the cell from outside was one of the main occupations of the locals. The cell was very dirty and strewn with bits of dirty cardboard. There was plenty of insect life on the floor and walls and quite large cockroaches were evident. I collected the cardboard to sit on as there were no furnishings in the cell. I sat down to take stock of the injuries to my feet and legs. When I removed my stocking I found it soaked in blood. Two of my toes were in a mess but there appeared to be no broken bones. My left ankle was swollen and blue. My left knee was also swollen. (I was troubled with this ankle and knee for months afterwards). I had many cuts on both legs but these healed quickly. The back of my right hand was lacerated where I had fallen at some time and the nail of the little finger was hanging by a thread of skin. The remaining nails were discoloured by the blood underneath them. I was bruised and stiff all over. I dressed, and knocked on the door. After some time a guard came to the door. He spoke only Portuguese and seemed moronic. I mimed to him that I wanted to go to the lavatory, to have a bath and to wash some clothes. He showed no interest. He just closed and locked the door in my face.

I thought I would wait a little longer and have another go. Before I did so the door was opened and two armed policemen beckoned me to go with them. I was taken to an evil-smelling, filthy urinal and after that to a long shed which contained about twenty 'showers'. All these were dripping water and the broken floor was awash. I selected the 'spray' under which I was going to shower and then tried to find a dry spot to place my clothes. I had no soap or towel but decided to use my singlet and pants to dry myself and then wash them afterwards together with my wollen stockings. The guards remained at the only door. When I turned the water on all the showers came on together and my clothes on the floor were soaked. I rushed to pick them up and put them outside the door. The two guards roared with laughter at the antics of a naked white man dashing about. It was now getting very dark and I obviously had to get a move on for the guards were getting impatient and kept shouting at me in Portuguese. I had a quick shower and dressed at the door, leaving off my vest, pants and one stocking. I would have to try and get these washed in the morning.

When I entered the cell I was surprised to see that I had company. Sitting on the floor with their backs to the wall were five black prisoners: three elderly men and two younger ones. My 'seat' of cardboard had disappeared and I could see that they had shared it out between them. They also had blankets, two each, and bundles of old clothes. I was not unduly worried at this for I was to get a bed and mattress and since this cell obviously could not hold it I would be elsewhere. I leant against the wall to await developments. Some time elapsed and the door was again opened by the regular gaoler. He had a plate of *sadza* covered with some greasy substance and a mug of water which he placed on the floor just inside the door. I immediately went into a mime indicating that I wanted to be taken to my bed and mattress but he looked at me blankly and closed and locked the door. I drank the water and gave the *sadza* to one of the elderly blacks. Just after this they spread the cardboard on the floor and made their beds on it using their bundles as pillows. Soon there was snoring from one of them. We had not exchanged a word. I was beginning to get worried about the long night ahead. I was very tired and thought that if only I had two blankets that would satisfy me. I certainly did not like the idea of lying directly on the concrete floor with all the insect life there. Later — I judged the time to be about nine p.m.—I again banged on the door, much to the annoyance of my companions in the cell who took rather a poor view of being awakened. Eventually the gaoler opened the door and after I had repeated my miming performance he made it clear that I was going to get nothing further that night: no blankets, no bed. So much for that damn captain. No doubt he had been trying to raise my morale also and had not meant what he said.

I suffered another dreadfully long night but not as bad as the previous one in spite of the wet clothing. About an hour after dawn the door was opened and the blacks trooped out leaving their blankets and packs behind. I took the opportunity of asking to got to the 'latrina'. Again I had to wait until two armed guards were mustered and I was taken to the filthy urinal. I indicated that it was a little more serious than that and I was led to the back of the barracks to an open space of rough grass. Parallel to the rear wall of the building and some forty metres away from it was a long trench about fifty metres long and five metres wide. It was very deep. About ten metres apart were narrow planks across the trench. There was no cover and the only shelter from the public gaze was the wall of the barracks on one side and a semi-circle of car and lorry wrecks on the other side. The guards indicated that this was the place to use. It appeared one had to stand on one of the planks then squat and perform. In my physical state I did not think I could trust myself to remain on the plank and had a horrible vision of falling into the trench which appeared to have been much used. Perhaps I could manage with one foot on the bank and one on the plank but then I decided that I had lost the urge and would defer the operation. I had brought the singlet, pants and stockings with me and washed them under the tap outside the urinal.

Back in the cell again I proceeded to make myself more comfortable by lying on the blankets left behind by the other prisoners. At the window I could hear people stopping to look through the holes. I must have dozed for suddenly I noticed the sun was strong and high and I was reminded that the clothes I was wearing were very damp and also that I had washing to dry. I banged on the door and when it was opened indicated my wet clothes and that I wanted to go into the sun. The gaolers had changed and this one seemed more agreeable. He indicated that I must wait and closed the door. A little later it was opened again and in the care of two armed guards I was led into a small yard in which a wooden seat had been placed in the sun. I spread my clothes and myself and relaxed. About midday I was visited by a senior police officer but again no English was spoken and this time no smiling interpreter attended. This was most frustrating for I had so many questions to ask. After he left it was indicated that I was going to move. I collected up my clothes and followed one of the guards with the other close behind me. We walked about five hundred metres to another gaol! The cell I now entered was smaller than the previous one but equally dirty and foul-smelling. It had no light and the walls were covered with writings (in Portuguese) and obscene drawings. 'Viva Frelimo' was on one wall in very large letters. The door was ill-fitting and had dropped on its hinges necessitating a noisy struggle when it was opened or closed. It was now secured by a heavy chain and padlock and because of this I had about three minutes warning of the door being opened. That afternoon it was opened many times, once for a greasy meal to be put inside the door and several times for men, women and children to view the prisoner. Again I had no blankets for the long, cold night.

In the afternoon of the following day I was ordered outside and taken to the gate of the prison yard. Here I found a Landrover with two guerrilla commanders and five guerrillas waiting to receive me. I recognised the guerrillas but the commanders were new to me. I was almost glad to see them! I was told to get into the Landrover, the floor of which was covered with weapons over which a blanket had been thrown. There was a large drum of diesel behind the driver's cab and this had leaked onto the floor. I was told, in English, to sit beside the drum while the two commanders got in front beside the driver. The remaining four guerrillas got into the back with me. Outside the police barracks where I had first been taken we stopped to pick up two guerrillas who also got into the back. (I did many trips in Landrovers during the next six months. Always we were cramped and grossly overloaded and each time there was a leaking drum of diesel oil.)

We made many stops on that trip and the commanders and some of the guerrillas got out to enter a house or store. Each time they came back into the Landrover they were more cheerful and less steady. I was left with three guards and these were usually handed a bottle, unlabelled, containing what looked like gin. I was offered a drink from this bottle but refused. Apparently it was a locally brewed alcohol and very potent. At one stop I was given a bottle of orange drink and some coconut biscuits. When we were on the move one of the commanders in front opened the sliding window between and tried to hold a conversation with me. I had difficulty in hearing and had to guess at his questions. From his reactions I was obviously saying 'no' when he expected a 'yes'. After some time and when he had made some calls en route, he gave up and went to sleep.

Many times we were stopped at Frelimo road-blocks and when this happened the side curtains were lowered and a blanket thrown over my head. None of the Frelimo ever looked into the vehicle. Some time after dark we left the tarred road and a little later started swerving along a track through trees. We travelled some distance before coming to a halt. I judged the time to be between seven and eight p.m. All curtains in the Landrover were lowered. After the weapons had been removed all the guerrillas left except for two who remained in the vehicle as my guards. I could hear a lot of movement outside and judged that I was now in the main camp at Chimoio. It was very hot and foul-smelling in the closed Landrover and I asked what was happening. I was told that we were waiting for a senior commander to come to talk to me. Some time later the back flap was raised and the head and shoulders of a big-built man appeared over the tail board. I could not see his face clearly but he appeared to have fierce eyes and a closely cropped beard. After he had chatted to the guards about me in Shona, he turned to me and said: "What's your name? Where do you come from?" The same old questions. And I gave the same old replies.

"Are you a mercenary or a member of the Security Forces?" he enquired with a certain menace in his voice.

"No," I replied forcefully.

"Did you enjoy your long walk?" he asked ironically.

"Hardly. You fellows walk too fast. I had to run most of the way." I then launched into a description of my hardships on the march and mentioned that I had suffered some injuries. No one, however, had given me any medical treatment.

"That's no problem. A doctor will see you tonight. Is there anything else you want?"

"Yes, I want a bath," I said truculently. "And can I write to my wife? She should know that I am still alive. And I would like my pipe and the medals they've taken from me. What use are the medals to your guerrillas—they can't eat them nor should they wear them. I would like them back." The commander said nothing. I continued: "I am a British citizen, you know. I wish to see the British Consul in Maputo."

The Commander burst out laughing. But he did say: "Alright, I'll see what I can do." He then spoke to one of the guards in Shona, told me he would see me again, and left. Throughout this exchange I had heard a peculiar rasping sound like pieces of leather rubbing together and I assumed that he was wearing a new shoulder holster. After he had gone I asked his name and was told that he was 'Comrade' General Tongogara who commanded the ZANLA forces. (ZANLA was the 'army' of ZANU). I enquired also about the rasping noise and the guard replied with a laugh that Tongogara always spoke like that. It was his teeth grinding together! I was told to get out of the truck and feeling in the dark for my pants, vest and stockings which I had carried rolled up, was upset to find that the singlet was missing.

I was taken into a large hut in which there was an enormous double bed made up and was told to sit down by four guards who then waited at the door. A man came in with a bag in his hand. He was wearing a white coat and proceeded to wash my damaged feet and examine them and my legs. He then informed me that the ankle sprain was a bad one but there was nothing seriously wrong elsewhere. No bones were broken in the left foot. He dressed all the cuts and bandaged my toes and, after questioning me about my health, left. I do not remember ever seeing him again, although it was dark in the hut and I may well have met him later without recognising him. He might have been a qualified doctor but more likely was a senior medical orderly.

A number of commanders came into the hut one after the other, introduced themselves, and asked the usual questions of me. As I have said, it was very dark in the hut and I could not see their faces or remember their names. About this time a meal was brought in consisting of *sadza* and chicken plus a mug of water. After I had indicated that I had finished eating I was handcuffed to one of the guards and taken to another hut. Here there were eight or more guerrillas lying on the floor smoking cigarettes and listening to a transistor. The handcuffs were transferred to one of these guerrillas. About an hour later as we were settling down to sleep a girl entered the hut with a small tin bath and hot water and told the guards that I was to have a bath. She then fetched a small towel, some toilet soap and a large piece of foam as a mattress. The handcuffs were removed and the guards took up position at the door. I had a very welcome wash all over and then again was handcuffed to one of the guerrillas. I started off lying on the piece of foam but in the night found myself on the earthen floor with my handcuff-companion lying on the foam mattress. He was much bigger than I and I left it at that. In the early hours of the morning (I later learnt that it was four a.m.) I was awakened and told that I had to leave the hut. The handcuffs were removed and with an escort of about ten guerrillas I walked about three or four kilometres into the bush surrounding the camp and spent the day there; I returned to the hut at about seven or eight p.m. The handcuffs were only worn during the hours of darkness. On the first morning, before I left the hut I asked to take the towel, soap and mattress with me not knowing I was to come back but was assured that they would be there when I returned in the evening. However, I never saw them again and it was seven weeks before I was given another small towel. This procedure continued for nearly three weeks before a small grass hut was constructed for me, and later a grass bed was added. I longed for sleep but slept very little, day or night. The guerrillas were obviously quite content to sit and talk to each other but I wanted activity or occupation to take my mind off my desperate situation.

After retiring from a very active life how had I got myself into this mess? I thought back to 1973 when Jennifer and I had been living comfortably in the northern suburbs of Johannesburg some twenty kilometres from that congested city. We had both travelled to our offices each day and both were subject to the stress and strain of driving in the rush hour each morning and evening. The rush hour in the morning is from 7 a.m. until 8 a.m. and in the evening from 5 p.m. to 6 p.m., but only residents can recognise it: to visitors it appears to last sixteen hours a day. The twenty kilometre journey used to take an hour and fifteen minutes and one arrived home exhausted and in a foul temper. I am sure that the traffic congestion of Johannesburg is mostly responsible for the high alcoholism rates of the area. It is said by the residents that they only live in Johannesburg in order to save enough money to go and live elsewhere. Certainly the standard of living of the whites is very high and there is much evidence of "keeping up with the Joneses." We both hated Johannesburg but stayed because we loved the theatre and the classical concerts which were more available there than elsewhere in South Africa.

Our holidays then were usually spent in Lesotho in the calm and beauty of the Maluti Mountains. We used to stay in a rondavel in the grounds of the Blue Mountain Inn at Leribe and walk, motor and ride in the foothills of those attractive mountains. However, after self-government and the building of the Holiday Inn with its casino the atmosphere changed rapidly and we had given up going there. We had already gone through the same experience with Swaziland. One day we both agreed that we had had enough of the rat race. It seemed madness to suffer the present discomfort for an uncertain future. I had been on a tour of Rhodesia some two years before and had fallen in love with the country and its people, both black and white. I had particularly admired the Eastern Highlands area—Inyanga, Umtali and Melsetter—with its mountains and forests. I remembered the scenery there as being some of the finest I had ever seen and the climate was exhilarating. Jennifer had not accompanied me on that first trip and we therefore decided to take leave and confirm if I still thought the same about life in Rhodesia. At this time there were already guerrilla activities in the north east, the Mount Darwin—Centenary area, but the Mozambique border was still open and there was no trouble there. People living in the Eastern Highlands still made their weekend trips to Beira for prawns and other sea foods.

In May 1974 we had set off by car from Johannesburg. The road from Johannesburg to Beit Bridge runs through very dull country as does the road from Beit Bridge to Bulawayo but we enjoyed the lack of traffic on the roads. We had no set plans but stopped when we felt like it. We enjoyed the Victoria Falls, Lake Kyle and of course Salisbury; but once again I fell in love with the Eastern Highlands. Surely, to live and work here must be heavenly, I thought. Jennifer agreed wholeheartedly.

We decided to return to Johannesburg and make the

necessary arrangements to leave and move as soon as possible to Rhodesia. We had noted that furniture made in Rhodesia was of good quality and design and reasonably priced. We had therefore decided to sell our heavy stuff in Johannesburg and travel light with crockery, cutlery, bedding and personal possessions. For this we needed a robust station wagon with a large roof-rack. Cars and trucks in Rhodesia were in short supply and very expensive. Back in Johannesburg we gave notice to all concerned and bought a new Peugeot 404 station wagon with a large roof-rack. In July we were ready to go and set off.

After about three months in a furnished flat in Mount Pleasant, Salisbury, we had made for Umtali. In Umtali we first rented a furnished cottage at the Christmas Pass Hotel but mostly ate at the Wise Owl Motel as the Christmas Pass Hotel was for sale and due to close. Meanwhile we were making enquiries regarding suitable properties in the area which would give us the surroundings we sought with an income from fruit and vegetable growing. We decided that as we were newcomers it would be wise to rent with a view to purchase so that we could have a good look at the prospect of viability. Eventually we leased a property of about one hundred and forty acres known as 'Little Go'. It belonged to Alan Constable who was then working for Air Malawi. The property was occupied by Air Commodore Frank Hyland-Smith and his wife Audrey, both delightful people who gave us a first class hand-over. We could hardly have foreseen at that time, indeed, how significant our acquaintance with them was to prove. Himself retired from an active career in the Royal Air Force, Frank Hyland-Smith's initiative in later writing to the British Foreign Secretary on my behalf had, I believe, considerable bearing on the timing and nature of my release.

After a month or two we had realised that we could not make a living from that property and Alan Constable, who now lives in Salisbury, generously released us from any obligation. He and his wife Florence became our firm friends and were a great comfort to Jennifer during later troublous times. We had already decided that a neighbouring property known as 'Listonhaugh' would suit us fine. It had been used for vegetable production before and had a large soft-fruit orchard plus citrus and avocado trees. The house was single-storied, well constructed and quite large, with two bathrooms. Although the grounds were neglected (the previous owner had been dead for two years and the two black caretakers had not worked very hard) I welcomed the challenge to get it into full production again. There was a lot of growing timber and a delightful lake. In addition we had marvellous views of the Mozambique border. We could also catch glimpses of Lake Alexander, and the colourful scene as the sailing boats competed at the weekends. We fell in love with the place and decided to change the name to Rustig*. This had been the name of a small property I had owned in the Eastern Transvaal.

Before moving in we had been given two bitch pups of uncertain pedigree which we named Mitzi and Olga. Their dam was a pedigree bulldog which had obviously had many lovers, for the pups were very unlike each other although they were from the same litter. Later we were given a third puppy by Mrs Hunt of the Vumba. This puppy was a yellow labrador bitch and we named her Anna Katinka. She was a lovely natured dog, almost human in her understanding of our moods and re-

* Afrikaans: Peaceful, quiet.

57

quirements. Like most Labradors she was remarkably easy to train. She loved me to take a .22 rifle and go out shooting the numerous guinea fowl on the estate. The other dogs, Mitzi and Olga, hated guns and also disliked horses. They would never follow me when I was riding. We also owned a cat, Tiddles. She was beautifully marked and a great personality. She loved to walk with us and the dogs until she became exhausted and had to be carried. Being a great hunter she more than earned her keep but infuriated us by bringing all her captures into the house alive and then letting them go so she could play with them. We spent much time recovering them from inaccessible places behind the fridge and wardrobes. She, meanwhile, had lost interest and gone out to capture something else.

At this time we had to make a trip to Johannesburg to arrange finance to purchase the property, to buy a second vehicle and to make other purchases such as a deep freeze, etc. We quickly discovered that because of U.D.I. and financial restrictions we were going to be under-capitalised and we had to be content with buying furniture and farm equipment from Umtali auction sales.

The district in which Rustig is situated is known as Odzani. It is about forty kilometres from Umtali along a winding road with many hairpin bends. The whole area was given over to plots like ours on which semi-retired people grew fruit and vegetables and did some dairy farming. Our nearest neighbours were Gordon and Merle Bradley about three kilometres to the north, and Strace and Pat Stroud about the same distance to the south. Already many properties in the area had been vacated but the people remaining were kind, generous folk who made us very welcome. Beyond the plots and small farms the area was given over to forestry, mostly pine and blue gum. There was much wattle but at that time it

58

appeared to have no market value being used mainly for firewood by the black Rhodesians.

Our first and most important task had been to mend or replace all the fences round the vegetable plots for in this area we were much troubled by bush pigs. I was to find out the hard way that they also liked fruit and would break down the branches to get at the plums and apples. In addition we had other marauders. I remember clearly that, one Sunday morning when Jennifer and I had climbed to a kopje overlooking the property which offered us a marvellous view, we could see movement in the orchard. After a time we could distinguish a troop of baboons moving from tree to tree, each taking a bite at a fruit and then throwing it on the ground. They seemed keen on the quinces but still took only one bite at each fruit. We were very frustrated for we were too far away to prevent this wasteful damage and the dogs were with us. Anyway, good fences would not keep them out. Later we were to be troubled by night apes known locally as bush babies. They would strip the green mealies.

The wild pigs were very cunning and a menace throughout Rhodesia. They did much damage to my place digging up the youngberry and raspberry plants and also eating the potato crop. They would eat the potatoes from under the plant without disturbing the tops, and until the haulm started to turn yellow and die back one would be unaware of the loss unless a close examination of the crop was made. Many times I rose long before dawn to lie in wait for them but never once did they come near me. This was a common experience with many of my farming friends. One morning at about 8.30 I was walking with the dogs, carrying a .22 rifle on the chance that I might encounter some guinea fowl. The three dogs entered a thorn thicket barking madly and emerged after some time being chased by a large boar accompanied by two sows. Olga and Mitzi came rushing back to me but when the bush pigs turned back after sighting me Anna attacked the rear of the boar. He turned and pinned Anna to the ground and in desperation I fired at his head, not expecting to do any damage with a .22. However, I was in luck for the shot penetrated his eye though it did not kill him. He dropped on his chest and made the most awful noise. Anna made good her escape and I went up to finish off the beast. The two sows left the thorn thicket and galloped off. The boar was a big one and it took four of us to get it back to the area of the dwelling. Eventually we managed to hang it from a tree. It looked repulsive and was covered in ticks. I told my 'boss boy', Kenneth, he could have it. He was overjoyed and two nights later about thirty of his friends joined my labour force and they had a feast.

How long ago it all seemed now; a figment, almost, of the idyll we had enjoyed so briefly. Here in the sticky heat of the thick bush surrounding Chimoio it seemed a very distant time indeed.

3

During these three weeks I received treatment for my left foot and for diarrhoea. This latter treatment came about in a significant way and confirmed my suspicion that every move I made and every word uttered was noted and reported by one of the guards. When one desired to urinate one was allowed to walk a few metres away and perform but it must never be close to a tree. If the requirement was of a more serious nature I had to ask for a *'badza'* with which I walked to a spot some distance away as indicatd by the guards who accompanied me on my mission. I then dug a hole. There were no supplies of toilet paper, for the guerrillas used leaves or grass; but in my present condition I did not think these were suitable. I was reduced to tearing out the lining from my jacket and converting it into small squares. Once finished I then filled in the hole. As I have remarked I had severe diarrhoea but nothing was said. Two guards stood close to me throughout. The following morning when the medical orderly came to treat my damaged toes he remarked that he understood I had diarrhoea and gave me some tablets! The medical orderlies were always well supplied with vitamin tablets, pills, medicines and bandages, usually of Chinese origin. Their only 'instrument' was usually a razor blade, which could be used both for sharpening a pencil and for lancing a boil—and probably was.

About this time I learnt that there were two other

white prisoners near me but I was not allowed to talk with them or even see them. I often wondered as to their identity for I knew of several whites who, like me, had been abducted after which followed silence as to their whereabouts and condition. After I was allowed into the grass hut I learnt their names from a note written by one of them, Jon Kennerly, and passed to me hidden in a small tin of brown sugar. The other prisoner was Johannes Maartens. In the same note I was given some hope of an early release by the information that on the radio which Kennerly had been given there had been reference to a statement of the British Consul in Maputo that he was requesting the Mozambique Government to give him my location and state of health, but had had no response. Again wishful thinking asserted itself and I was pleased to assume that I was being kept apart from the other prisoners so that I would not be able to say much about them if I was released in the near future.

These were dreadful days and nights. I felt ill and with nothing to do thought all the time of what might have been. How stupid not to have moved from the border when we had talked of doing so months before. How was Jennifer and where was she? It was impossible for her to continue with the farm; surely she would leave that dangerous area now that I had been taken. Would she move into Umtali or go to Pretoria to live with her brother and sister-in-law? How about our dogs, Mitzi, Olga and Anna Katinka? We were both devoted to them and I knew that Jennifer would not easily part with them and would never have them put down. I cursed myself for giving her so much worry and anxiety. Would it have been better if I had been killed? Surely better than for her to have to wait not knowing if I was alive or dead or if and when I would return. And then if I was killed, would she ever be notified? I thought not. And so it went on. I was obsessed with worry for her and the guerrillas became quite concerned about my 'low morale'. They used to say "You must resist, resist. It's the situation, it's war." I was to hear this said to me many times over the next six months when ill or exhausted after a forced march. I used to ask them what they knew about a real war. Soon it became apparent to me that there was no point in dwelling on past mistakes. It was water that had passed under the bridge. I must survive the present and try to keep fit for the future. All my efforts must go into that and I agitated to be allowed to take exercise and once again tried to eat the awful food.

One afternoon whilst still in the bush and before moving into the grass hut I noticed my guards suddenly springing to their feet and straightening their clothing. A large number of armed guerrillas was approaching and behind them came 'Commander' Tongogara and his staff including some women 'commanders' in neat uniforms. The guerrillas encircled me and Tongogara then asked me yet again about my health and requirements. To those I had mentioned before I added that I wanted reading matter, a toothbrush, soap, towel, comb and a razor. I also asked to see a Red Cross representative. As I spoke he nodded to various members of his staff who busily took notes. At the same time he was saying to me. "That's no problem." (I was to hear that assertion from commanders at all levels whenever I made a request. It all seemed very efficient; but it was months before I got a towel, toothbrush, comb and toothpaste though I learnt later that it was no fault of Tongogara's that the items were so slow in coming.) My requests recorded, he went on to say: "The British Consul has been on to me twice already. He wants to know where you are and if you are well; but I will not tell him where you are. You have got to stay here with the comrades. You must live with them and share their life in the bush. It will not be easy for you."

Throughout our discussion he kept addressing me as 'Major' in a heavily sarcastic way. Then the whole procession moved off in the shape of a half moon with Tongogara and his staff behind the leading guards of the escort. Their dress was not uniform but the senior commanders, both men and women, were well turned out. Some carried brief cases and tape recorders. All were armed.

The following morning I was handed some reading matter in the shape of three old copies of the *Zimbabwe News*, a bi-monthly magazine of the ZANU Party printed and published in Maputo. It was of course full of propaganda and some of the accounts of incidents and attacks in Rhodesia were grossly exaggerated, but it was well produced apart from many errors in the spelling. In the absence of anything else I read it. I was also handed a razor, three blades, a mirror and a tablet of toilet soap. I started to shave but the blades were Tanzanian and of very poor quality and I used two before I had shaved one side of my face. Before I could progress further a guerrilla arrived to take away the razor, blades and mirror. I protested that I had not finished but he was adamant and said that the commander wanted them at once. Obviously giving me the blades was a mistake. I might cut my throat or wrists—for surely they did not think I could attack eight guards with a razor blade! However, I was never given a razor or blade again although I later discovered that young Jon Kennerly had both and he had hardly started to shave. However, by that time I had grown a beard. Although this was hot and uncomfortable it did give some protection against the insects, particularly the mosquitoes.

In the afternoon I was again placed in the middle of a single file of eight guards and we moved off further into the bush. Some 400 metres after leaving my 'hiding place' I passed an old bell-tent with a fire burning outside. I was told that this was where the other two white prisoners lived. However, it was empty at the time. We walked deeper into the bush for about two kilometres and then halted under some trees. The guards took up position round me. Faintly I could hear someone talking and a little later much clapping and shouting from many voices. Whoever it was was hidden from me. A short time after this I could again hear voices faintly but closer to me and in a different direction. They were in a hollow and out of sight. And then suddenly a large number, about 30 or 40, of armed guerrillas appeared and approached me in a semi-circle. They encircled me and my guards withdrew. Within the centre of the half moon formed by the escort was a group of men and women all armed, some carrying brief cases. In front of them walked one unarmed figure, impressive in appearance. He was short but squarely built and was well turned out in a safari-type suit with a long-sleeved jacket and long trousers. I recognised him as Robert Mugabe, President of ZANU. He came to within two or three paces and spoke to me in good English and in a quiet voice.

"What is your name and where were you farming?" he first enquired. After hearing my reply, he asked: "Have you any immediate problems?"

"Yes," I replied. "I want my wife to be informed that I am still alive; I would also like to be put in touch with the British Consul in Maputo as I am a British citizen."

He made no answer to this, but said blandly: "I understand you do not eat *sadza*."

I told him that I did not like any soft, sloppy food; that in fact I had tried to eat the *sadza* but could not keep it down. I preferred my food to be dry. With a business-like nod, he turned to one of his aides and gave the instruction that I was to be given some biscuits and tinned fish.

During the course of this exchange one of his commanders broke in and reminded me that I was talking to the President. Apparently I was not showing enough deference. I replied that I was aware of who he was as I had seen many pictures of him.

At the interruption of one of his staff the President had held up his hand to check the commander. He then asked me what else I wanted. Before I had time to reply he said: "I know what you most want—your freedom; and so do I."

With that he turned away and the escort and command party moved off. As they moved off I recognised Josiah Tongogara, Josiah Tongamira and Joshua Misiharambwi whose pictures had appeared in the *Zimbabwe News*. Some I had met on the night of my arrival at the Chimoio headquarters. My guards closed in on me. I immediately thought of all the other things I should have asked but I had not been prepared for an interview with the President.

He had certainly impressed me favourably with his quiet, courteous manner, mostly I suspect because of the entirely different picture I had of him from what I had read in Rhodesia. I realise that our talk was brief but my impression was that he was a sincere man dedicated to his purpose. Sometime before this he had publicly stated that he was an avowed Marxist. I often wondered if he regretted making this speech as it gave his opponents the opportunity of labelling ZANU a communist party. This was often put forward as a reason the West should oppose the Patriotic Front and support the internal set-tlement. I do know that many commanders in ZANLA stated that they were not communist and did not sup-port a Marxist policy. I know also that Tongogara wrote and also said in speeches that he was not a communist. Most politicians and leaders regret at least one speech in their careers. Did Robert Mugabe regret his 'Marxist speech'? As the Eastern Bloc countries were supplying ZANLA with arms and ammunition, perhaps he had been diplomatic. The unusual thing about all this was the Mr. Mugabe was reported to be 'a devout Catholic'.

I was still spending my days in the bush and being handcuffed in the camp at night. However, one day I was told that from that night I would occupy a small grass hut which had been constructed nearby. From there I could see the top of the bell-tent housing the other white prisoners. The following day a grass-covered bed was constructed on wooden posts. I was glad of this for some insect, a spider or a scorpion, had bitten me during the night and I had a painfully swollen finger. Both spiders and scorpions came in all sizes. Some of the spiders were enormous and had large bulging eyes. Snakes abounded and for some reason not clear to me they were not to be killed in Mozambique. It was amusing to see my guards trying to shoo them away. At this time it was still quite cold and the snakes were sluggish. Up to now I had had no blankets of my own and the first night in the grass hut I was given one blanket. Some weeks later I was to learn that this blanket was not an official issue to me but had been given to me anonymously by one of the guards from his issue of two. A kind gesture for which I was never able to thank him. The following day I was official-ly given a lovely coloured blanket which had just been washed. I now had two blankets and a grass bed, the height of luxury. And what was more agreeable was that the handcuffs were no longer used. I still had eight guards under an elderly man who called himself 'Comrade Weber'. All the guerrillas had given themselves *Chimurenga** names and they were addressed by these names preceded by the word 'Comrade'. Oddly enough these names were in English and some of them were strange indeed. Off hand I can remember Comrades Bazooka, Hyaena, Trymore, Blaster, Takemore, Margo, Killer (ominous to say the least), Everyday, Alfred, Trevor, Alpha, Macdonald, Seduce, Tokyo, Justin, Enoch, Africa, Samora and Darlington. Their proper first names were also usually English names like Charles, Thomas, Richard, Kenneth, etc., but they did not seem to use these although the senior commanders retained theirs. The use of 'Comrade' was obligatory and when one thought about it, very convenient. The guerrillas had no badges of rank and so if a guerrilla appeared on the scene who was not known to them the use of 'comrade' got them out of difficulty. Although they saluted commanders at all levels, usually by stamping their feet and, if armed, by carrying the weapon under the left armpit and bringing the right hand across the body with the tips of the fingers touching the weapon, the use of the word 'Sir' was never used. Their use of the word 'commander' always confused me for they applied it equally to a section leader right up the scale to 'General' Tongogara who commanded the ZANLA forces. When I met a commander I never knew the level of the man I was addressing although I learned to recognise some of the higher commanders whose

* *Chimurenga* was the name applied to the rebellions against the white settlers in the 1890s. It was used again to describe the modern guerrilla war. *Chimurenga* roughly translates as 'freedom fighters' but it also has the historical connotation of the ancestral spirits who were thought to have urged the rebellions of the 1890s and the guerrilla war.

photographs frequently appeared in the *Zimbabwe News*.

The guerrillas were always cheerful, talking and singing throughout the day and most of the night. Their singing in unison I found most attractive but individually their repetition of two or three notes sung in a high falsetto was irritating. They also had many *Chimurenga* songs and sang these continuously. Not understanding Shona I asked for the words to be translated. Much later I was given the words in English and I print them here.

For the Freedom Fighters
Alongside the Zimbabwe fighters,
The liberators of Namibia,
The fighters of Western Sahara,
The struggling people of Palestine,
The heroes of South Africa,
A struggling-front, to close ranks
Afro-Arab peoples, joined hands:-

Chorus
The freedom of peoples, independence of countries,
For prosperity, peace and unity,
The struggle so wages, for rights and equality,
Let it strengthen its anti-imperialist stance,
Let it strengthen its anti-colonial struggle.
And long live the struggle of all the freedom fighters.
To intensify the struggle for freedom,
To crush and destroy colonialism
And imperialism to fight,
(The) oppressive system to unseat,
Freedom's torch to light,
The Afro-Arab peoples proved valorous,
Their solidarity emerged victorious.

WHEN GUNS FIRE

When guns fire, they remind me of our Fatherland Zimbabwe.

Our parents are being harassed by the Boers in Zimbabwe.

These things remind me of our Fatherland Zimbabwe!

Collect the mortar and recoilless rifle, then let us go to Zimbabwe.

These things remind me of our Fatherland Zimbabwe!

We are staying in the caves and mountains because of Smith.

We are staying in the caves and mountains because of Chirau.

We are staying in the caves and mountains because of Sithole.

We are staying without clothing and food because of these people.

 Our parents have all died.

They make detente so as to finish our relatives.

Most of the guerrillas had a copy of Mao Tse Tung's *Little Red Book.* I had heard of this book for years and I asked for the loan of a copy for I was desperate to read anything to take my mind off my depressing situation. However, none of them would let me have his copy.

One of my guards, Gerald by name, was very musical and made himself a guitar. He often played a tune which sounded very similar to *Amazing Grace,* but said that he had never heard of the title. He was quite a skilled performer which is more than can be said for dozens of others who strummed on the instrument. Gerald had been wounded in the left foot some months before this and the wound was still suppurating. He never complained on the marches but I noticed he took his left boot off at every opportunity.

They loved to tell stories about their recent employers in Rhodesia and were good mimics, taking off the voices and mannerisms of 'madam' and the 'boss'. Their audience was usually convulsed with laughter and asked for more. This story-telling would usually start about nine p.m. and go on into the small hours.

If one complained about anything the answer was always the same: "It's the situation; it's war. You must resist, resist." They themselves seemed to welcome discomfort and hardship, regarding it as a test of their manhood.

My guards had a fire burning at the entrance to my hut and this often filled the hut with smoke. The main purpose of this fire during the day was to provide lights for their cigarettes but was used to warm them at night. At night no flames were permitted—only a red glow, and they were skilled at sustaining the embers in this way. They smoked continuously using uncured leaf which they dried on the ashes. They were always short of paper for their cigarettes and would sometimes be reduced to peeling strips of cardboard. The smell of the burning paper and tobacco leaf was unpleasant but they seemed to prefer these homemade cigarettes to the machine-made variety. My pipe, taken from me after I crossed the border, had been returned to me with a small quantity of manufactured tobacco. After this was finished I tried some of the uncured leaf but this gave me terrible heart-burn and I decided I had better give up smoking. Later I was sometimes given packets of cigarettes of Mozambi-quan origin and these I stripped down for use in my pipe. Many of the cigarettes meant for me were 'lost' on the way. I did not resent this for after all I was their prisoner and they themselves were often without tobacco of any kind.

About this time I had a visit from a guerrilla who claimed to have just returned from a 'mission' in Zimbabwe. He also claimed to have worked for me and although he had knowledge of my other labourers I did not recognise him. I think he must have met my employees at the farm. He told me that he had visited my homestead about midnight one night and that Jennifer was still there 'living with' a man, either a policeman or soldier, as he wore uniform. I asked how he could find out all this at midnight and he said that my labourers had told him. I did not believe him of course, but confess this report troubled me for I had nothing to do but think, think, think, all day and all night. This was a psychological attack as they had long realised that I worried a great deal about Jennifer's safety and whereabouts. I was always pestering to be allowed to write to her or tell her I was alive and reasonably well. They resented this and advised me to forget her. In addition they added that *their* wives and families had been left behind and that they had had to forget them. Some of them had been guerrillas for about ten years and they had not seen their families throughout this length of time. Later I was to receive other false reports about Jennifer but it had become obvious to me that they were trying to soften me up so I ignored them. I would ask them about my dogs for I knew that where Jennifer was the dogs would be. This usually proved to me they were lying for they were unable to give any information about the dogs.

4

After about three weeks my feet and legs were almost recovered although my toes still required treatment. This recovery came just in time for without prior warning I was awakened one morning before dawn and told to hide my blankets and scant personal effects in the long grass and get moving. These effects consisted mostly of tins for boiling water on the fire and plastic bottles for holding drinking water, plus some biscuits and tinned fish. All these items had been 'come by' over the weeks and were invaluable to a prisoner in the bush. Justin, the guerrilla who came to move me, was a security commander. I disliked him intensely for he was constantly ordering me to "Move. Move. Move now," always without warning even though sometimes he was in the vicinity for up to an hour before he gave the order. When I sighted him I never knew whether to prepare to move or not. Invariably I lost something on these panic moves and we walked into the bush in the dark, often through bush-fires, and returned to the hut at last light. On these moves, which went on almost daily until we left that area, I often caught glimpses of Jon Kennerly and Johannes Maartens who were also on the march each day. It appeared that an air raid was expected and everyone was being moved. Where possible we walked along the dry river beds to avoid the bush fires and often came across the wild animals looking for water. There were all sorts of buck in the area but mostly we saw baboons. I remember one particularly large male baboon who appeared to be more like a gorilla. His companions were in the edge of the bush but he had found a pool of water and was loath to leave it when we approached. He would retreat a few paces and then dash back bellowing all the time. The leading guerrillas in my column levelled their weapons at it but I knew they would not fire as this would create consternation among the others in the area. Eventually they drove the baboon away with a hail of stones. I fully expected him to start throwing them back.

There were hundreds of baboons in this area and many of them lived on a rocky kopje some half mile from my hut. I often heard them calling to each other and sometimes I could hear them fighting. The bush around us had been burning for days and the noise from the crackling of the fire and falling trees was very loud.

One evening at about eight p.m. a tremendous uproar broke out from the kopje. The fire had reached its base and was slowly and inexorably burning its way to the top. The baboons realised that they were trapped and were screaming with fear and rage. It was some hours before the volume of screaming decreased to an occasional bellow of defiance. The next time I was able to view that kopje in daylight I saw that there was no sign of green vegetation. I wondered how many if any, baboons had escaped the flames.

The bush fires were a constant worry. Sometimes when I was being hidden under cover during the day I would hear the crackling of the flames all round me getting closer and I had visions of being burned alive. Often I would be moved hurriedly through the gap remaining. How these fires originated I do not know. I had heard that through carelessness there had always been many 'grass' fires in Mozambique. The guerrillas told me that these fires were started by the Rhodesian Selous Scouts. Later when being marched through various areas of Mozambique the burnt countryside smelt very strongly of paraffin and I thought that some sort of 'fire bomb' had been dropped by aircraft.

These days were boring and we were driven mad by the flies. Most of the trees were deciduous and looked very grey and dead. Because of this we were made to hide under bushes. Once in position no movement was allowed. Water was always short as this was the height of the dry season, just after mid-winter. However, near my grass hut was the river and there was still sufficient water there to be able to say that it was flowing and drinkable. It was in this water also that we bathed, the three white prisoners (separately of course) and the guards who accompanied us. One of the maddening things about these days spent under the bushes was that when you returned to your base in the evening there was no fire, no water, you wanted a bath and you had to find your belongings in the long grass. Food did not worry me providing I had some of the 'issue' biscuits which I used to stuff in the pockets of my jacket before moving off in the morning. By this time I had kindly been given a 'towel' by a guerrilla named Samora. It was a small sack which had contained brown sugar and still had suger adhering to it. I opened the sides and whenever anyone went to the river I asked them to soak it. At first it was like rubbing oneself with sandpaper but it eventually softened. I still had a remnant left at the time I was released. Up to then I had borrowed a towel from Jon Kennerly whenever I could get a bathe in the river. Of course I never saw him about it but the guards would arrange it. Later on when he lost his towel I returned the compliment by giving him half my sugar sack. Another thing I acquired at this time was a spoon. It always bothered me to have to eat with my fingers, particularly in getting fish out of a tin. One day the guerrilla named Takemore brought me a teaspoon with about an inch of handle. This was a boon but I found difficulty in getting to the botton of the fish tin. I asked him to fit a wooden extension to the handle and this he did, binding it with a string from a mealie meal sack. Later we were each given a desertspoon but I kept my teaspoon until the end and have it to this day. Sometimes our meal of rice and *sadza* and fish was delivered by two girls from the main camp some distance away. They would also sometimes take away clothes for washing. Often they would reject the clothes saying that they had no soap. They would never wash our underpants for apparently they would only do that for their husbands.

One day, I think it was a Sunday towards the end of August, we did not go on our long walk. I was visited by a junior security commander who told me he was going to fetch another white prisoner who had spent the previous night in the bush nearby. He said that the new prisoner was a helicopter pilot. Later that morning whilst I was trying to persuade a 'logistics' (supplies) commander to take a letter for posting to Jennifer I was joined by James Black from Melsetter. He looked very rough and somewhat haggard. He told me that he was not a helicopter pilot but a forester in Rhodesian government employ and had been 'taken' in Melsetter some eight days previously. He had spent six days in the same gaol as I had been in Vila Manica and we were able to exchange views on that horrible place. Anyway he was spared any 'solitary' in the bush for he stayed with me and we shared the little hut for the next few days before moving out into the bush never to return to it. The following day the hut was enlarged and two beds were constructed, though it was about three weeks before

Black was given any blankets of his own. We managed with one each, plus a few clothes we possessed. He had recently been on two months' leave in England and the Continent and had returned only four days before his capture. Whilst in the U.K. he had read in the London *Daily Telegraph* of my being abducted. We had much to talk about and conversed into the night discussing the details of our capture and the routes along which we had been taken into Mozambique. We also talked of the dreadful conditions in the prison at Vila Manica and our prospects of surviving. From what Black told me of the dangerous situation of the whites in Melsetter the situation in the Eastern District of Rhodesia was rapidly deteriorating.

The area around the hut was becoming polluted for although the guerrillas were very keen on bodily cleanliness they knew nothing or cared nothing about 'camp' hygiene. Food was left lying about covered with flies, uneaten food was thrown into the undergrowth, empty and half-empty fish tins were just thrown away without being buried and so on. In addition we were all using the area for calls of nature without latrine pits or the use of lime. I pointed out to the commander of the guards, Weber, that we would have an outbreak of typhoid or dysentery if we went on like that. He agreed but nothing was ever done about it. Before we finally left the area both Jim Black and I saw large numbers of rats closing in on the bivouac area and the flies were like swarms of bees. Although the guerrillas had the opportunity of taking anti-malaria tablets they were never forced to do so and many of them went down with malaria. They did not seem to get any treatment but were left alone in their blankets until they recovered. They regarded malaria as Europeans regard a heavy cold.

One afternoon before Jim Black joined me, a girl came to my hut carrying a recent copy of the *Zimbabwe News,* which she gave to me. She sat on the bottom of my bed and said she was a secretary in the main camp. Because of my bandaged feet I was lying on the bed without shoes or socks. She began stroking my feet and ankles and murmuring: "You poor thing." I got very worried and started to move to the top of the bed. However, she continued. The guards were around the entrance to the hut and were very amused by all this. After a while the guard commander returned and spoke sharply to her in Shona, apparently telling her to clear off as she was out of bounds. She casually said goodbye and wished me luck, then sauntered off as if she was crossing Cecil Square* or somewhere similar. Although the male guerrillas were poorly off for clothing and were often in rags the women seemed to be well dressed. They always seemed deliberately to wear clothes too small for them so that their bottoms were obtrusive and their navels exposed. They always wore slacks.

Up to now I had had much 'casual' questioning but no really heavy interrogation. Almost immediately after his arrival Jim Black was interrogated in the grass hut. I was sent outside whilst this went on and was unaware of the questions and answers. After they left he had to write out his life story from first starting school. The next day they started on me. There was usually a team of three interrogators but some members changed over the months. However, the chief interrogator remained constant: he was Commander Lamec and he claimed to have received his intelligence and psychological training in China over a period of about five years. (He was a Black with eyes like a Chinese; we spoke of him as 'Wun

* Cecil Square is in the centre of Salisbury

Lung Hi'). He was very proud of this training and considered himself an expert in human psychology. Personally I was not impressed with his interrogation methods or with his line of questioning and Jim Black agreed with me. His method was to give us pen and paper and get us to write out our life history from starting school up to the day of our capture. Dates of everything that had happened to you were most important and also details of military training and campaigns in which you had taken part. This was a terrific chore for me. I was over sixty and had been a regular officer in the British Army for fifteen years and a regular officer in the Royal Air Force for ten years. During my service I had of course undergone much training and had served in many parts of the world. I could not even remember the month and year when I started my primary school! I started off by deciding to condense all this and to say nothing of my fighting the Chinese communists in Malaya for three and half years in the 'fifties'. This item would not have helped my case against the 'mercenary' charge. I had to guess at some of the dates and this later almost proved disastrous.

These lengthy autobiographies had to be written out under the most difficult conditions and they were in a hurry for them. Often one would have to move in the middle and try to complete it while crouching under bushes. Always one thought that the completed document might have a great bearing on one's future! When it was completed Lamec collected it and took it away for studying by all three of the 'team'. They would then return with questions. During these I would be taken apart from everyone else and be alone with the three interrogators some two or three hundred metres away. Questions over, I would be sent back to the guards and heaving a sigh of relief would tell myself that that was not too bad but thank goodness it was over. Little did I realise that the ordeal had only just begun. This was August and my interrogation was completed in October.

Presumably the completed 'history' was taken to a higher authority, for some time was to elapse before I saw the team again. Then one day they appeared with pen and paper and asked for the whole thing to be done again! My heart almost stopped beating. What about all those dates I had had to guess at? I asked if I could copy the original. They looked at each other and laughed, saying that they had not got the original and would I get a move on. They would come later that day to collect the papers. This was shattering. Because of the mercenary charge I had re-arranged my personal history to exclude all reference to the period in Malaya and also had been rather casual about dates; so casual that I could not remember what I had written. Was my life to depend on this report? I overcame my panic and got to work. By dark I had not completed the dossier for I was having trouble remembering those dates I had given. However, I was lucky for a change and it was two days before they returned to collect the completed papers. This was probably due to the fact that we had moved again.

Some days later they returned and this time they had both copies. I was again taken aside and then began a most uncomfortable interview. It appeared that the two copies did not agree one with the other and they were interested—to say the least—to know why! They went through both copies line by line. I pointed out that I was over sixty years of age and that it was difficult to remember exactly when one had started school or when one had undergone certain training. At times we became angry with each other and voices were raised. You must remember that at this time I was not feeling too well and for their part they were convinced throughout that I had been engaged in helping the Security Forces before my capture. Eventually I was sent back to join Jim Black and the guards. I was feeling more dead than alive.

It appeared that we had left the grass hut near the main camp in Chimoio for the last time as we were carrying all our possessions. We had a fresh sleeping place in a valley near a dry river. This was a dreary place and every night a mist would settle over the area. The whole area had been thoroughly burnt and any movement brought forth clouds of ash. The ground was very uneven and much worse was the smell of dead animals, caught in the fires, whose carcasses were rotting. Because of our constant movement food supplies were irregular and usually cold and stale. It was very cold and very damp. On 1 September 1978 an air raid by the Rhodesian Air Force took place and bombs were heard exploding but not very near to us. Before first light each morning there were hundreds of people on the move including ourselves. We often saw the other two white prisoners with their escort, sometimes in front of us, and sometimes behind us; and although we were close enough to wave to each other we were never close enough to converse. We also observed large numbers of black prisoners being escorted out each morning, and back at night. However, they were never 'camped' near us. Again water was a problem. There would be no rain for months yet and we were reduced to drinking water that looked like used motor oil and seemed full of insect life. We had been given bottles of orange squash locally brewed and called *Sumovit* to help improve the drinking water. The guerrillas called it 'Mazoe' after the Rhodesian orange squash of that name. This was a great boon and we particularly valued the plastic bottles the squash came in for we were able to carry water in them on the long marches and the days in the bush. Some of the nights were so cold we could not sleep in spite of all our exercise during the walks. On these occasions Jim Black and I would sit by the small fire.

One night an incident took place which kept the guerrillas amused the next day. One of the guards named Takemore used to sleep next to me when not on sentry duty. His ability to snore very loudly bothered me for I am a light sleeper. One night a large male bush pig came into our sleeping area and stood over him making subdued snuffling noises. It was driven away but the guerrillas were convinced that it had mistaken the snores for the cries of a mate and Comrade Takemore was ribbed mercilessly. This Takemore was the same man who had given me the spoon. He was a great trencherman and usually started eating before the others and finished well after them. One day quite by accident I addressed him as Eatmore and his comrades thought this a huge joke and often they addressed him as Comrade Eatmore. However, he did not seem to bear any grudge. Obviously my thoughts had been transmitted to my tongue.

I often found that my memory played tricks and one day I got into a panic because I could not remember the names and addresses of relatives and friends with whom I had been corresponding for years. During my interrogation I had acquired—stolen—a ball point pen; I kept it hidden for we were never allowed to have a pen or paper except for the purpose of writing our history or writing a letter, after which the pen and paper were removed. When I realised that my memory was failing me I took to secretly writing down names and addresses of those near and dear to me when I remembered them. I used the inside of cigarette packets for paper. Later I acquired some pages of a school notebook and wrote down all the poetry I could remember. I never did manage to remember all of Kipling's *If.* What I did remember of the hackneyed poem sustained me often, particularly the lines "If you can meet with Triumph and Disaster and treat those two impostors just the same . . . " There were few poems that I could remember completely and I would try and exercise my mind by compiling my own lines to fill the gaps.

5

We never knew and were never informed if we were to return to our 'nightbase' when we set out each morning and so we always carried our possessions on the long walks into the bush. Sure enough one night we did not return but made our 'base' in a far better area under some large trees standing in a park-like setting.

It was here that I noticed that the guerrillas used a piece of wood from a particular bush for making a toothbrush. I asked them to show me how to do it. They took a piece about six inches long, broke off both ends, and chewed one end until it resembled a paint brush; they then used the brush-end on their teeth. It seemed to work well as a 'dry' cleaner and it was to be a long time before we were given proper toothbrushes and toothpaste.

We were only in the new site for a few days and during this time we stayed put day and night. On Friday 8 September we observed a large gathering coming towards us preceded by the usual half moon of armed men. We were being visited by Commander Emerson and his staff. His full name was Emerson Munangagwa* and he was special assistant to President Robert Mugabe. I found him a pleasant, cheerful man with a marked sense of humour. He had spent many years in

* Emerson Munangagwa became Minister of State when the Government of Zimbabwe assumed office in April 1980

detention in Rhodesia and whilst there had studied for and obtained a law degree by correspondence with London University. He sat down on a blanket under a tree and spoke to us saying that we were to have been released but the bombing by the Rhodesian Air Force had put paid to all that. Before he spoke he had attempted to use a tape recorder but it would not work; they were always using tape recorders. (After we were released the suggestion was made in Rhodesia that we had broadcast on Maputo radio. This was untrue and I can only think that one of the taped conversations or interrogations had been broadcast.) In his entourage were men and women staff officers and a photographer who proceeded to take photographs of Jim Black and myself both individually and with Emerson. We thought this a good sign. Perhaps the Red Cross were pestering for proof of our being alive or perhaps a copy of the pictures would be sent to the *Herald* newspaper in Salisbury. In either event our families would be informed of our state—that is if they could recognise me in that beard. He then asked if we had any requests, and in addition to the usual ones for towel, toothbrush, etc., I asked for a transistor radio and to be able to write a letter to Jennifer. We had the usual reply—"that's no problem"—and his staff were told to do something about it.

We (Jim Black and I) also asked if we could meet the other two white prisoners who were camped some four hundred metres away, for by now I was sure we would not be released ahead of them. Again, he said: "That's no problem," and sent for them. When they arrived we introduced ourselves and practically fell on each other's necks. Emerson watched quietly, rather amused it seemed. He then broke up the touching scene by repeating to Jon Kennerly and Johannes Maartens all that he had

85

said to us and telling them to have their photographs taken.

This done he said that we would soon be on the move and he prepared to leave us. (From this meeting and our conversation I got the impression that some negotiations had been going on regarding our future but that whatever ZANLA had planned for us had come to naught. Apparently we were now no longer going to be kept close to the main camp at Chimoio but moved deeper into the bush.) I reminded him about the letter and he thereupon ordered his secretary to collect four pens and some paper from amongst the guerrillas present and we set to writing whilst he waited without any show of impatience. I wrote to Jennifer and told her amongst other things that this was my second letter. During my captivity I wrote five letters which were taken for 'posting' and this was the only one that reached her. What Jennifer actually received some months later was a photostat copy posted from London! There was a page missing. Was that some crude form of censorship or just carelessness?

It was amazing that here Emerson was, sitting with us in the bush in full battle rig, but shortly after we heard that he was in London in a five-star hotel. These guerrillas were becoming much travelled, and not only the senior ones: often we heard of quite junior commanders who had received training in Russia, China, Rumania, East Germany or other Eastern European countries. Many hundreds had received training in Tanzania. Robert Mugabe was the most travelled of them all and seemed to spend most of his time journeying from conference to convention drumming up support for the Patriotic Front.

After Emerson, his staff and escort had left us we resumed our talking with Jon Kennerly and Johannes

Maartens. We heard the story of their capture and experiences to date and they listened to ours. We heard these stories repeated over and over during the next four months and eventually became heartily sick of them. Only our own story never seemed boring.

Jon Kennerly was the first of the four to be taken. In February 1978 he had hitched a lift in a lorry going to Beit Bridge from Bulawayo to see his parents who had recently moved there from Bulawayo. Just outside Beit Bridge the lorry was stopped by guerrillas and Jon was taken off. There were two blacks in the front of the lorry with Jon but they were unharmed. They were told to say nothing about the incident but to their credit they reported it to the police in Beit Bridge. Jon had had a long and arduous walk along the Limpopo River before crossing into Mozambique where he was transported by vehicle to Chimoio camp. At one point he tried to escape, had got away, but was recaptured when he went to a river for water after being overcome with thirst. After this escape his captors took away his boots and bound his wrists behind his back until he reached the vehicle. Jon was only 17, very tall and slim and quite good-looking. He was very popular with the guerrillas and they made much fuss of him. Every commander that came to visit us knew Jon and made a beeline for him. I got to know him very well and we became good friends in spite of our difference in age. He called me 'Uncle'. For some obscure reason, just after his capture, he was advised to say that he was a member of the Rhodesian Light Infantry, a unit of the Rhodesian Army. This he did and no doubt it caused him some worry during the interrogation sessions. In point of fact he had never served, being too young. At our first meeting he was drawn towards James Black and they spent much time together. They were the two youngest although Black at 45 was old enough to be his father.

Johannes Maartens was South African-born and aged 55. He had been a farmer all his life and had not travelled very much. Born in the Orange Free State, he came to Rhodesia in 1947. He farmed in the Headlands area, growing tobacco and fattening cattle. Before his capture he had taken the precaution of moving his family into the nearby town of Rusape. He had seven children and they were a very close-knit family. Some years before he was taken he had undergone major heart surgery in Groote Schuur Hospital in Cape Town, being attended by Professor Chris Barnard and his team. He was covered in scars and was still regarded as an invalid by his family. He was a simple, brave, kind and cheerful man much strengthened by his Christian beliefs. He believed everything the guerrillas told him and in this respect we thought him naive. On the day of his abduction he had visited his farm from his home in Rusape. He had arrived on the farm at about eleven a.m. to find the guerrillas there. They stayed on the farm with him all day whilst he supervised the packing of tobacco for the auction sales. They told him also that he would be allowed to go after they had talked with him. However, just before six p.m. they left the farm taking him with them and set off on the long walk to Mozambique. This was in May 1978. This walk must have been quite a struggle for him but the guerrillas were conscious of his condition and rested when he asked them to do so. They looked after him well and when we met he seemed quite fit and able to undergo the long marches without too much discomfort. His belongings were always carried for him by one of the guerrillas but he had acquired a heavy overcoat and with the pockets filled with biscuits and orange squash I discovered that his coat weighed as much as my sack of belongings. He was very attached to a rancher's hat he was wearing when captured and in spite of its becoming dirty and battered he kept it throughout his imprisonment. Fortunately for him he loved *sadza* and always had a good appetite, eating the *sadza* with his fingers. His Afrikaans was better than his English and with his beard and rancher's hat he strongly resembled pictures I had seen of Voortrekkers before the time of the Boer War. Jon Kennerly and Maartens had been together for some time before we met and Jon called him 'Oupa' which is Afrikaans for grandfather.

Jim Black and I provided our two guests with a meal of biscuits and fish followed by black tea from our supplies. We also listened to the news for the first time since our capture, as Jon Kennerly had been given a transistor radio some time before and had brought it over to us. The afternoon passed all too quickly as we out-talked the guerrillas, which was quite something. Some time before five p.m. the guards of Maartens and Kennerly said they must now return to their bivouac. We objected and eventually prevailed on the guards to wait until we had heard the six p.m. news. It had been quite a day, with the profitable visit of Emerson and our meeting with Jon and Johannes.

I think it was the next night we heard the news of the shooting down of the Viscount and of the massacre of the survivors. What a tragedy. This would put back any question of an all-party conference and would stiffen the resistance of Rhodesians against any form of compromise. Any criticism of Smith's Government would be stifled. The Patriotic Front would get no kudos or gain from this infamous act. Our guards, one of whom had heard the news on Jon's radio in the nearby bivouac, were jubilant; but later I was to hear from a senior commander that he thought the incident had harmed their cause. I think it was another crime like the Elim Mission massacre that was possibly carried out by a local commander without higher authority. No doubt the aircraft was shot down with the approval of Nkomo but I do not believe he ordered the massacre of the survivors. However, his heartless acknowledgement later was in appalling taste and he forfeited the right then to be treated as a responsible leader.

The following morning Emerson proved as good as his word and we were handed a rather worn, much-battered transistor radio. I had asked for this so that we could hear the news in English from South Africa and Rhodesia but later I was many times to consider it more of a curse than a blessing. Whenever we switched it off to conserve the batteries the commander of the guards would ask for it either to listen to Shona music or the news in Shona. There were many 'liberated' radios about but our guards never seemed to get one. That evening at eight p.m. they took the radio to listen to their own news programme from Radio Maputo. This was a ZANU-sponsored programme of heavy propaganda. After this Shona dance music came over and they started to dance dressed in full rig and holding their weapons. They became quite drunk on the music and danced and sang quite frantically. Jim Black and I had curled up in our blanket under the trees but as we were in danger of being trampled on we got up and stood by the fire until the hysteria died down. We were both quite nervous and did not know what to expect. Quite often we had to ask for the radio to be given back in order to listen to our news. Some of the guards resented our having it at all but did not seem to object to our listening to the news in English when we did have it. They themselves would crowd round the set to listen to the news and would cry out "Lies, all lies" when the Combined Operations' reports were read out reporting the deaths of many guerrillas in Rhodesia. In some ways the guerrillas were very tolerant; or perhaps they were slow to react. I remember that one Sunday morning we were listening to a military band programme and suddenly the march *Sweet Banana* came over loud and clear. This is the regimental march of the Rhodesian African Rifles, the guerrillas' sworn enemies. There was a sudden hush from our guards followed by a lot of muttering and hostile looks. I expected them to come and snatch the transistor away.

Although we were close to a river there was little water and having a bath presented difficulties. All water for cooking, drinking, and bathing had to come from a rather dirty-looking 'water-hole' in the dried-up river. Quite rightly no one was permitted to bathe in the hole: instead an enamel wash bowl was produced and this was filled by scooping out water with a tin from the water-hole. One stood, naked, on a rock and used an empty fish tin to scoop water from the basin and pour it over one's head and shoulders. One then soaped the head and body and used the fish tin to rinse off. If there were two of us we rinsed each other. The guerrillas used this method also and usually at the same time. I noticed that they were well-built and proportioned and thought there must be something in this *sadza*, their staple diet, after all. I also envied them their beautiful teeth which seldom saw a toothbrush or toothpaste.

Three days after Emerson's visit, on Monday 11 September, we were on the move again. Jon Kennerly and Johannes Maartens joined up with us and we set off walking, accompanied by about twenty guards. We walked about five kilometres to the outskirts of the main camp at Chimoio. There we halted to await transport to a new location. Whilst we were waiting we were given tea and I was given some cigarettes. The guards were changed around and later we realised we had some new faces and others that we had met previously. Some of these new guards were quite young, in their teens, and were to prove difficult to get on with. We had noticed that the older men were more patient, kind and sympathetic towards us whilst the attitude of the younger ones was that here they had four white 'bosses' at their mercy and yet they still had to wait on us with food and water. We would have preferred to have got our own food and water and even have a go at the cooking but this was never permitted. Once we reached a bivouac area we were not permitted to move about except to go for a *badza* trip, under escort.

After a time we were led to a Landrover on a nearby dirt road. The vehicle was already half full before we got in, with the usual drum of diesel and various sacks of meal. After we had climbed aboard only two escorts armed with AK 47s could get in and we were appalled to notice that one of these was Comrade Lamec! Obviously more interrogation was planned for the immediate future and this fear was increased when I noticed him carrying his briefcase, the sight of which always made me feel nervous. The other escort I had not met before and we were not reassured when he was introduced as Comrade Killer. He was a junior commander employed on 'logistics' which meant he was responsible for supplies and the day-to-day running of the bivouac area. As is not unusual with anyone engaged on quartermaster duties he was always better dressed and better fed than anyone else. We were to find that cigarettes and additions to our rations such as potato crisps and the odd tin of fruit did not get beyond him. In the front of the Landrover, beside the driver, was the camp commander of Chimoio. I think his name was Tuli. The rest of the guard detail, about twenty guerrillas, would have to walk.

We had not travelled far before we pulled off the road into the bush and were told to dismount. We had reached a ration dump and we had to make room for some more sacks of mealie meal. Everything was taken off and re-packed. We squeezed on again and drove about 30 kilometres along little-used tracks. At one point we met a guerrilla convoy going in the opposite direction and the commander in front stopped to speak with them. We were told that they were the 'mortar party' returning from the attack on Umtali and we were given a graphic description of the havoc they had caused and the hundreds they had killed! I thought: "Jennifer surely must have left Umtali by now."

When we reached our new area we were all rather down-hearted. It was the site of an old hunting camp and the area abounded with the skins and skeletons of dead animals. The smell was overpowering and maggots and flies were there in abundance. Rubbish and the remains of old fires were everywhere and the only hut was in a sorry state and absolutely alive with insects and rats. We started to object to staying there but it was unnecessary as Tuli told Lamec that we were to be taken further into the bush, nearer the river. After unloading the Landrover we were called together by the camp commandant. He addressed us as follows: "You are about to start a new stage in your imprisonment. You will live the same as the comrades and learn of their hardships and way of life. You will not get any privileges but sometimes you will get additions to your food as I know you do not like *sadza.* If you do not do as you are told it will be the worse for you." He then addressed us separately saying: "Have you anything to say?"

When my turn came I said: "I want to contact the British Consul. Can we have books to read and playing cards? We were promised towels, soap, comb and toothbrush, but have not received anything."

He replied: "The question of the British Consul is a matter for the High Command. I cannot do anything. As for the other things—that's no problem. I will visit you soon."

He got into the Landrover and was driven away. In the absence of any other guards we were told to move the offloaded rations to our new area, a distance of about half a kilometre. Whilst doing this we were closely watched by Comrades Lamec and Killer.

Later that afternoon the rest of the guerrillas marched in, hot and weary. They were not in the best of moods and we kept out of their way as far as we were able. We were told that there was plenty of water in the river and we would be taken down for a bathe that evening. All the guards that could be spared had already gone down to the river. They loved to bathe and spent hours over it if possible. When we later went down to the river we discovered that it was wide, almost dried up, but with quite large pools and even flowing water. A static pool had been set aside for the washing of clothes and we were given washing soap for this purpose. We spent a very enjoyable hour here and Jon Kennerly managed to swim about 30 metres. By this time his hair had grown down to his shoulders and he wore a decorative head band. Sometimes he wore his hair in a pony tail. He took great care of his head and body and amused everyone by shampooing his hair. Where he got the shampoo from I do not know but Jon had a lot of treasures from his early days alone when he was quite spoiled by the guerrillas. After all, he was much nearer their age group than we were.

Among the guerrillas guarding us was a medical orderly whose name was Enoch. As usual he had plentiful supplies of vitamin tablets, bandages and medicines but no instruments. We badly needed scissors to cut our toenails, finger nails and beards. My beard was very full and bushy and was growing upwards on my lower lip. My moustache was getting long and growing downwards. The two lots of hair were in danger of merging and I found eating a messy business. Amongst his comrades Enoch seemed a very untypical guerrilla: very much mixed-up, he made himself a nuisance to us because he so badly wanted to be liked and could talk the hind leg off a donkey, with the consequence that he always outstayed his welcome. He was inclined to be lazy and sometimes would keep us waiting for hours after he had promised to treat our cuts and so on. Sometimes he would go off to a local hamlet and after a couple of beers (presumably) he would return singing and giggling like a young girl and make himself a nuisance. He appeared to be devoted to Jon Kennerly and would put his bed next to Jon and talk into the night but we all grew to dislike him and called him 'The Mopani Fly'. He came from Umtali and had received his medical training in Mozambique.

Our bivouac area was near a rocky outcrop overlooking the river. The worst thing there was the flies. They came and settled on us like swarms of bees and head and shoulders would be covered with them. When you heard them coming the only thing to do was cover yourself with a blanket.

The second night we were there Commander Tuli from Chimoio drove in quite late with some extra rations for us including a bag of glucose sweets which he gave to Jon. He had obviously stopped en route for refreshments and had difficulty in keeping awake. The following day we were given a new towel each but they were only of hand-towel size. We were also given a good supply of toilet soap. That evening we moved again further away from the river. We did not move very far and were to continue to use the river for bathing and the washing of our clothes.

Our commander at this time was one MacDonald. He was very taciturn and I do not think I exchanged more than a few words with him in the weeks we were together. Even during the subsequent resumption of the interrogations he never spoke. He never gave us an order direct but always via Lamec, Killer or a junior commander who called himself 'Seduce'. However, one night he asked me if I had been to China, I replied in the affirmative and he told me he had been trained in China and liked the Chinese. MacDonald, Lamec and Seduce formed the interrogation team. MacDonald was always well turned out and ready for immediate action. He would have made a good regular soldier and appeared to have no soft spots. He was remote and spent hours on his own reading what appeared to be law books.

Some two or three days later after this last move things took a turn for the worse. We were awakened early and told to hide our belongings under bushes or in the long grass. We were then conducted into a dry gully or ditch and made to lie down. The ditch was under trees and had good overhead cover. The guards took up position on the banks and we were not permitted to move about. We stayed there during the daylight hours and it was very unpleasant for the ditch was teeming with insects of every variety. At last light we were ordered out and walked about fifty metres to where we had to sleep in the open. We suffered from stiffness and cramp. The next day the performance was repeated.

Sometime during the morning we noticed that the guards all had their boots off and were examining each other's feet. Jon asked them what they were doing and they said that the whole area was alive with jigger (or sand) fleas and they were trying to remove them. I had heard of jigger fleas for my brother had suffered from them in the Sudan. We were informed that to start with they merely caused itchiness but they rapidly multiplied and consumed you flesh. We four decided that our feet were itching and that we should do something about it. The guerrillas showed us some they had removed from their toenails. They were white and about the size of a pin head. You really needed a needle to remove them but no one had a needle, not even Enoch, and the guerrillas brought us some long thorns like the ones they were using. And then started a long painful process which was to last for many days. We had already been able to deal with our own lice and every morning went through a delousing period during which we removed one garment at a time and as well as the lice to try to get rid of the eggs. Only a hot iron could do that effectively for they seemed to thrive in cold water but these jigger fleas were a much greater problem. To start with they burrowed under the toe nails and unless you got extremely close to the foot you could not see them. The second problem was to get them out without breaking the egg sac to which they were attached. Jon volunteered to be our medical orderly and did sterling work for which he deserved a medal. He studied the methods of the guerrillas and learned to recognise the little fleas and where they were usually to be found. He then went to work on his own feet and quickly found some under his toenails and in the soles of the feet. We had been told that the recovered jigger fleas must be burned or they would hatch out a new brood. We could not do this, not being allowed to move and so Jon placed them on a leaf (they seemed to be quite static at this stage) and when the leaf was covered it was folded carefully and taken to the fire by one of the guards. Having completed his own feet Jon would have a go at ours. He was very good at this and very patient when we snatched a foot away—for the probing with the thorn was often very painful. I did not much care for messing about with my own feet and certainly could never have coped with someone else's so I admired Jon for this. We suffered from these jigger fleas for many days, for long after we had left the area Jon continued to dig them out. I remember that in one session he removed 25 from my two feet. Five of them were under one toenail and the resultant wound from the thorn gave me much trouble. Equally painful were the sores caused by removing them from the soles of the feet.

6

We were doing this first-light-into-the-ditch, last-light-out-of-it routine for days before the air raids by the Rhodesian Air Force started again on 20 September. They lasted three or four days. In addition to the jet aircraft, helicopters were used to land ground troops and to provide extra fire power. On Thursday 21 September at about 2 p.m. six helicopters flew low over our heads just clearing the trees above us. They landed beyond us and there was much firing of machine guns and mortars. They appeared to be landing troops for after about half an hour they took off again and flew back in the direction they had come from but to our flank.

Our guards closed in. For the first time they were joined by Commander MacDonald who took up his position a few metres from us. It was apparent to all of us that if the Security Forces approached close to us we were likely to be killed by our guards and no doubt the attacking forces would be blamed. However, the firing was moving away from our position and we stayed put until last light when we slept in our usual place in the open about fifty metres away. No fires were permitted that night and the guards were all on duty around us. Throughout that night we could hear mortar and machine-gun fire. The next morning long before first light we were all on the move away from the direction of the previous day's firing. However, MacDonald was no longer with us and it was some time before we saw him again. We thought he had been killed. Commander Seduce was now in charge. We crossed the river and walked through burning veld into a sunken 'road' some six kilometres away. Here we spent the day.

I was to see here something I had never expected to witness. I suppose everyone can remember seeing a picture of their first school book showing two 'Ancient Britons' wearing skins trying to make fire by rubbing two sticks together. The guerrillas had discovered that no one had matches or lighters in our new location and they were all longing for a cigarette. In any case they always loved to have a fire going even on the hottest days. All that morning a pair of them tried to make fire. One would twirl the vertical stick while the other would hold the horizontal stick all the time blowing on it. It must have been the wrong wood, or damp, for it failed to ignite. Later, however, I was to see the method successfully applied. But the incident illustrates how feckless the guerrillas were, living only for the day and caring naught for the morrow. I had seen them lighting their cigarettes with matches whilst a fire burned at their feet: later they had neither matches nor fire. It was the same with carrying water on the march: we prisoners hoarded anything that would hold water especially prizing the plastic bottles which were best for this but the guerrillas would cut them to make cups and then throw them away after they had used them. If we had a surplus of bottles when we were due to move they would ask for them but never kept them once they were empty. They boasted that they needed to drink water only once a day. That was nonsense for often they would come to us for water during a long hot march. We sometimes had to refuse firmly for water was always difficult to come by.

At last light we set off back to our sleeping area of the previous nights. On the way we met many guerrillas moving away from the firing and fighting. When we reached the sleeping place where our belongings were hidden we had a quick meal of *sadza* and fish. We were then told to pack as we were going on a 'long' march. This was ominous for never before had we been warned of a 'long' march. As I have said, Maartens' sack was always carried by one of the guerrillas and, feeling very weak, I thought I would try to get them to carry mine. We both packed our sacks and filled our pockets with the hard biscuits and bottles of water laced with some orange squash. The transistor radio was not working and Jon hid it in some long grass. I placed my sack next to Maartens' and about eight p.m. we formed up in the single file ready to move off. Whilst we were waiting a hullabaloo broke out behind me. My sack had been discovered and they were looking for the owner. They brought the sack to Jim Black just behind me and said he was to carry it. I could not allow that and took the sack from him. We were all heavily burdened with all the unconsumed rations which had been shared out amongst the guerrillas and ourselves. They were always concerned about Johannes Maartens' physical fitness and would adjust their pace to his. We prisoners therefore always put him in front of us and told him not to walk too fast. We set off reinforced by other guerrillas who were leaving that area. The march that night was long and arduous. A large sack is not easy to carry on a long march for it gets lower and lower on one's back and one's arm gets cramp. A pack would have been much easier. We all fell down several times and on one occasion my green balaclava was lost. It fell off when I went down and I could not find it in the dark. The people behind yelled at me to "Move—Move. Get on" and so I had to leave it. I was rather upset at this loss for I had been given the balaclava just after my capture to hide my balding head and white face. It had served me well, keeping my head warm on the cold nights and, when pulled down over my ears, keeping out much of the noise by the talking and singing of the guards. Although often I was promised a replacement I was never given another hat although a cover would be placed over my head when we passed through kraals at night.

Maartens had a narrow escape that night when he fell into a sluice as we were passing through a farm 'owned' by the guerrillas. This farm was in very good shape and as well as vegetables and mealies had pigs and chickens. We had heard of it before and conjectured that we might be asked to work on it. Maartens, the enthusiastic farmer, rather hoped so.

During that night we saw hundreds of guerrillas on the move away from the fighting area and some of the senior commanders were waiting at the side to watch them go by. We marched until about four or five in the morning and when we came to a river we halted. We had covered about 40 kilometres and were very tired. Some of the guerrillas found a point where they could jump across the river and Jon Kennerly and Jim Black were ordered to follow them. This they did but the jump was too much for Johannes Maartens and me and with about ten guards we were told to lie down and wait for daylight. Later, after dawn, an easy crossing was found and we rejoined Kennerly, Black and the other guerrillas.

Then followed about ten miserable days during which none of us felt well. We were all stiff and had sore feet, and our bowels were giving trouble. In addition we still had jigger fleas in our feet. Our hiding place during this period was under some thorn bushes on a steep bank at the side of the river. We had to crawl into this place on our hands and knees and although we did some secret clearing we were never able to stand upright. The surrounding veld had been burned off, and the trees were leafless and looked most depressing, only the bushes on either side of the river retaining their leaves. We were obsessed with our bowel movements and enquired of each other after a *badza* trip like a worried mother with a constipated child. The impure water was the source of our trouble; and with constant movement it took some time for our stomachs to adjust to the changes. We had learned that what one suffered from today, constipation or the reverse, the others would suffer tomorrow. We coveted any sort of paper as toilet paper, particularly the labels off the tins, and quickly found the best label was the one from the tin of Dutch Mackerel. Only the two joining edges were stuck together and all of it came off in one piece. We found the young guards most uncooperative about '*badza* trips' at this camp and disinclined to accompany us. I solved this by not waiting for them if they argued about it and I would set off at a smart pace, forcing them to run after me to guard me: they would be in trouble if I were seen walking on my own.

As a result of the removal of the jigger fleas my feet again needed treatment and to make matters worse I received a bad scorpion sting on my left ankle which gave me trouble for weeks. We often had visits from the medical orderly Enoch but he seldom had his medical satchel with him. After some days without a bath because of the bombing or threat of bombing, we bathed daily here, going to the river at about five p.m. and sharing the bathing place with about ten or so guerrillas. I sometimes had to 'wash down' on the bank to avoid getting my bandages wet and the guerrillas thought this hilarious. After the bath came the meal, still under the bushes. Just before dark we were ordered to our 'sleeping place' still under cover but allowing us sufficient room to stand upright. There was very little room and we slept cheek-by-jowl with the guerrillas. However, the commanders remained apart and slept about fifty metres away. When Commander Seduce discovered that Jon had left the radio behind he was rather angry and organised a party of guerrillas to go back and fetch it together with some rations left behind in a ditch. Meanwhile we had been given another very old transistor which gave us the news. It seemed there were other camps of guerrillas in the neighbourhood for we received many visits from commanders we had not met before. Once again we had switched from frantic movements to complete inactivity but this helped our cuts and sore feet to heal. There must have been a village nearby for often some of the guerrillas would go off and return quite merry. On these trips they would leave their weapons behind. One afternoon two junior commanders came back from a drinking spree and spent an hour or so with us under the bushes telling us how lucky we were not to be shot. They could easily kill us and they need only write a report to say we had attempted to escape. No questions would be asked. They were quite 'high' and we were glad to see them leave. The conversation had been a bit one-sided.

My interrogation had continued over the previous two weeks and was to continue here as opportunity offered. It now took the form of question-and-answer and some of the questions exasperated me. Such questions as "What were Hitler's aims in the Second World War?" seemed to have not the remotest connection with my present situation. I was tempted to reply that Hitler had not kept me informed but Lamec's sense of humour was not up to it. The other thing that irritated me was that Lamec would start writing the answer down before I opened my mouth. He had preconceived ideas as to what the answer would be, and was furious if my answer differed from his. I suspected that his report would bear little relation to what I had said. I once asked if I could read my replies after he had written them but he refused. I was determined not to sign anything without first reading it. However, I was not asked to sign. One day he became exasperated when I hesitated over some fatuous question. He accused me of prevaricating or words to that effect and said I was trying to be clever. He would report me to higher command for being unco-operative. He tore up the paper he had been working on and ordered me to return to 'my comrades'. He seemed very angry. Another difficult time, I remember, was caused by my inability to remember details about the political parties in Rhodesia except for the Rhodesian Front which Lamec said he did not want to hear about. I suppose he had a right to disbelieve me for the initials of the parties (the UANC, ZUPO and so on) were always being mentioned in the Press and on the radio but I could not remember them. Throughout my interrogation Lamec would keep returning to the reason why I had chosen to live in Rhodesia *after* the fighting started. Presumably this was another reason why they were so convinced that I was a mercenary or had some connection with the Security Forces. I had already learned not to stress the fact that I was British and still holding a British passport. After my capture I had thought that stressing that I was a British citizen might help to secure my release but it was made clear to me one day in no uncertain terms that whites living in Rhodesia but not born in the country were regarded as 'bloody settlers' and beyond the pale.

Whilst we were here MacDonald rejoined us. He actually greeted us on his return and seemed pleased to see us.

Although the leafless trees resembled a petrified forest by day, when I was lying on my back at night the tops of the trees looked beautiful with the moon and stars as a backcloth. One night we saw the total eclipse of the moon and were asked to explain the phenomenon by some of the guerrillas.

On 3 October at about one p.m. we were ordered again to "Move—Move—Move." We were quite good at this panic-packing by now it took us only a few minutes. Blankets in the bottom of the sack; tins, bottles and any clothing we could discard on top of the blankets; biscuits and water in pockets, and we were ready. It was extremely hot. We did not walk far, only a few kilometres, halting at the side of a dirt road to await a large lorry. When it arrived we climbed aboard together with about twenty guerrillas. This was better than walking but our delight was short-lived for we were ordered to lie on the hot metal floor over the back axle, and were then covered over with evil-smelling blankets. The guerrillas disguised themselves as civilians and put their weapons on the floor of the lorry. We were obviously going to pass through Frelimo territory and we must not be seen; or perhaps we were not to see where we were going. It was a painful journey over rough dirt roads but I estimate not more than about 80 kilometres. I kept peering out of the blanket but could only see telephone posts and wires because the truck had high sides. However, I noted that we crossed the railway a couple of times. When we came to a halt we had to climb down and set off into the bush. For the first time I was told to leave my sack as it would be brought along later by the guerrillas. I was quite worried about this but grateful all the same, for I was feeling far from well with stomach cramps and felt bruised all over from the metal floor of the lorry. We eventually caught up with MacDonald, Seduce and Lamec who had gone ahead to select our next 'resting' place. Once again everyone was asking for water and so far no one had found any. The supplies we prisoners had carried were exhausted. Eventually a hole was dug and water seeped into it from a swamp area. This water looked and tasted foul but I drank it. That evening I felt very ill indeed and whilst the others were eating I sought my blankets. As usual we prisoners were sleeping in a row side by side with the guerrillas all round us and the commanders some little way apart. Some time during the night I was violently sick several times but I managed to keep it clear of my blankets. It was very painful, for my stomach was empty except for that foul water. I also had to make three *badza* trips and not knowing the topography of the area in the dark I kept tripping over sleeping forms and walking into bushes.

The guards were very patient and one of the commanders called out to inquire who was being sick. The reply was 'Papa Thomas' for that was what they called me. There was no sign of Enoch the medical orderly and nobody bothered to call him. In the morning I felt more dead than alive and hoped to 'lie in' but again: "Move—Move—Move," and we were off again. However, this was only a short move of a few hundred metres and we were again under bushes. With relief I spread my blankets and rested.

The following evening we were visited by Commander Rex Nhongo with another commander whose name I have forgotten. Rex Nhongo was Deputy Secretary for Defence and second in command to Tongogara*. He was popular with the guerrillas and had

* Rex Nhongo took over command of ZANLA forces after the death of Tongogara in January 1980.

quite a reputation as a good 'field' commander. I had not met him before and thought him less good-looking and fatter than he appeared in the many photographs I had seen of him in the *Zimbabwe News*. He was an ebullient type of man. He asked the usual questions about health and food and our requirements. Johannes Maartens asked for some chicken meat to 'relish' the *sadza* or rice (he asked everybody to get us chicken and sometimes it succeeded). I remember Jim Black talking of 'us chaps' and being smartly told by Nhongo that we were not 'chaps' but 'comrades'. After we complained about our clothing and footwear Nhongo said that was 'no problem' and that he would get us all 'new uniforms'. I thought that was a joke seeing that many of the guerrillas were in rags. I asked him when all this was arriving and he replied 'perhaps tomorrow'. That was always the reply. (I remember once being quite exasperated with this reply after asking for toothbrush, comb, etc., for the umpteenth time and I pointed out to the commander concerned that tomorrow never came; that at midnight it became today. Could he say that the items would come on Wednesday, Thursday or whatever and not 'perhaps tomorrow'. He loved this and roaring with laughter slapped hands with me. I again asked him when the items would arrive and laughing he replied 'perhaps tomorrow' and walked away. They were great jokers).

Later that evening after Nhongo had departed two live chickens were brought to us. He had fulfilled one of his promises. For myself I did not care for these Mozambique chickens. They were undersized, underfed, scrawny birds and I always agitated for them to be kept alive and fattened for a few days on the wasted *sadza* and rice before being killed. However, I think that Maartens worked on the principle of a bird in the hand being worth two in the bush and he was probably right.

108

He loved chicken, even the Mozambiquan type, and would suck the bones until they were white. In any case, at this time we never knew when we would be moved and it was unlikely that live chickens would be taken along.

By this time someone had discovered a river and we were told we could go and have a bathe. This was the evening of the day following Nhongo's visit. We set off with about eight guards and walked a considerable distance through burnt bush. It was very hot. I always knew what to expect on these occasions and I was not surprised when we arrived very hot and dirty at a small waterhole in a dried-up river bed. The water had been used for bathing and the washing of clothes by the guerrillas and the surface of the water looked as if it would have to be broken with a pickaxe. By the time we arrived back at the bivouac site we were more sweaty and dirty than when we had left. A bucket of water without the walk would have left us much cleaner. By the time we got back it was dark and after a meal of *sadza* and chicken we were told to prepare to move. This time we were to leave all our belongings behind except for our blankets. These would follow later with Lamec, in a Landrover. This was good news although at the same time it meant that there was another long walk in front of us. We set off and again put Maartens in front. However, this walk was shorter than before—only about 30 kilometres—and altogether easier without our heavy sacks although one or two river crossings were tricky in the dark. In the early hours of the morning, in the bush, we were told to get and sleep. All around us were hundreds of bodies lying down under the trees and it seemed that once again the guerrillas and their prisoners were all on the move. The next morning just after dawn we set off again but for only four or five kilometres. Here we were installed in a complex of rocky caves and outcrops where we suffered considerable discomfort from our cramped conditions. We were now in a long narrow 'passageway' between rock walls with an overhanging rock over its whole length. Its width was about one metre and for some unknown reason the commanders set up their headquarters at one end of the passage with all the rations and stores. At the other end was the entrance to this cave with the cooking fires outside. We were midway along the passage. There was much traffic between the 'headquarters' and the outside and everytime somebody passed along we had to stand up and let them go by. With all this rock and the confined space it was terribly hot and on top of everything else the previous occupants had dumped their unwanted food and tins in the crevices between the rocks. This had gone bad and smelt strongly, attracting flies and rats. Fortunately we were taken outside to sleep at night.

We still had commander MacDonald, Lamec and Seduce with us and for some unknown reason Jon, who had completed his interrogation months before, had to write it all out again. Perhaps it had been destroyed in an air raid or captured by the Security Forces. (We were to learn after our release that masses of papers and documents had been recovered from the main camp in Chimoio, including details of black and white prisoners). I was told by Lamec that some of my answers to a previous question session had been 'unsatisfactory' and that I would have to do them again. This was disturbing for some days before he had paid me a visit to say that I was now cleared of the charge of being a mercenary or assisting mercenaries. However, the following day we were moved and I never saw Lamec again.

7

The move this time, on 10 October, was accompanied by the usual last-minute panic, as (inevitably) the communications had broken down somewhere. At about noon we noticed Enoch rushing round gathering his bits and pieces. To our enquiries he merely replied that he was going somewhere. About an hour later one of the junior commanders came to ask why we were not packed and ready to move. This was the first we had heard of it. Apparently someone should have told us, probably Enoch. As no other guerrillas were going with us except Seduce, Enoch and six guards, we had not noticed any tell-tale signs of a move. After some shouting we moved off again into the hot sunlight.

I think at this time we were all suffering from 'running stomachs' and after about three kilometres of walking very fast I heard an an anguished cry from Jim Black me—"I've got to go in the bush"—and he fell out of the column followed by some of the guards. We eventually reached a Landrover and after handing over one blanket each were ordered into the vehicle. However, that was easier said than done for we were four prisoners with our sacks, eight escorts with their weapons and kit and the drum of diesel. The front of the vehicle was already occupied by the driver and our new temporary commander, Patrick, a sympathetic man who bought us oranges and soft drinks *en route*. The vehicle had to be offloaded and repacked which necessitated our emptying our sacks and stuffing the contents under the seats. We then climbed aboard for what proved to be one of the most uncomfortable journeys of my life—and I have covered hundreds of miles in tanks. We were like sardines in a tin and could not move a muscle once we were all settled. There was not room on the floor for all the feet so some of us had to put our feet on top of the others'. We had not gone far before Jon's head flopped onto my shoulder and I realised he had fainted. There was nothing I could do about it, for I could not move my arms, so I jerked my shoulder up and down to try to revive him, which it did. We had been on the move for about two hours when we stopped at the side of the road and were told to dismount. We marched off into the bush out of sight of the road and heard the Landrover drive away.

We had always learned that it was a waste of time asking what was happening, so made the most of the fresh air and tried to straighten ourselves out. After about twenty minutes we heard two vehicles return and we were then marched back to the road. The second vehicle turned out to be a long-based ambulance Landrover painted white with the usual red cross emblem on the roof and sides. From this ambulance a pleasant-faced man came to meet us. He introduced himself as Comrade Herbert and we then recalled that we had read in the *Zimbabwe News* that he was the ZANU Secretary for Health. His full name was Herbert S.M. Ushewokunze* and I had been told that he had had a flourishing practice in Bulawayo before he joined ZANLA. He told us that he was going to give us a medical examination and would start with Johannes Maartens. The rest of us

* Herbert S.M. Ushewokunze became Minister of Health of Zimbabwe after April 1980.

would wait under cover until called. I was told to strip to the waist and after the blood pressure test he said that I had high blood pressure and must watch it. This was the first I had heard of it but I was not surprised. I told him of my dislike of the sloppy food and my digestive problems because of it. He gave me a month's supply of tablets for high blood pressure and a supply of antacid pills for the stomach. Not long after this I accidentally left the blood pressure pills behind during a move but I continued to take the antacid pills as sweets. All of us got something except Jim Black who always seemed quite fit except for his irregular bowel movements. Of course Johannes Maartens got most pills and medicines and was producing his little bottles and packets after meals for weeks afterwards.

After the medical we squeezed back into the Landrover. We now had a female guerrilla in our company, but she sat in front with Commander Patrick and carried our medicines and pills. (We were so tight in the back we could not get the pills in without crushing them!) Then we set off for Tete which was about 300 kilometres north of that spot. On the way we made one stop for the calls of nature and to eat oranges, biscuits and sardines; also, I might add, to get the blood flowing again. Again we had to be covered with smelly blankets when passing other cars (very few) and passing through road blocks and villages. These road blocks were numerous even on the dirt roads. On the tarred roads they were usually sited at all entrances to towns and villages and at road bridges—presumably as a precaution against incursions by the Rhodesian Security Forces or the movement of the resistance force opposing Machel and his Frelimo government. They appeared to be very inefficiently manned.

We reached Tete at about 8 p.m. and parked outside

a house on the outskirts of the town. After some time we were taken inside and were met by Commander Josiah Tungamirai, the Deputy Chief Commissar. He was a cheerful character and we were to see much more of him. He told us that we would be given a meal and would then spend the rest of the night on the floor, to continue our journey northwards the following morning. During that evening he spoke to us at length about the 'situation' but did not ask us our opinion of things. He said that he had received a letter from a group of farmers in 'Zimbabwe' asking for an assurance that they would be able to reap their crops if they went ahead with the planting. (One of the many problems farmers in Rhodesia had to face, besides the fear of death or abduction, was that their labour was threatened with death or worse if they stayed to harvest the crops.)

We had a meal of *sadza* and fish washed down with orange squash and then got down on the floor. It was very hot and I found sleeping difficult. The climate in Tete is very humid and I made up my mind never to live there. The following morning we again climbed into the Landrover which was now parked at the side of the house. For some time the guards waited beside the vehicle and shortly we were to know why: General Tongogara was expected and would like to see us before we moved off. He came and spoke to us over the tailboard. He did nearly all the talking in those few minutes, though in the course of his remarks he asked Black all about himself.

"Who are you and where do you come from?"

"I am James Black. I was employed as a government forester at Melsetter."

"A forester. We need foresters in Zimbabwe. You should have been left to get on with your work."

Black was somewhat shaken by this, but was quick

to reply: "I agree. Perhaps you can arrange for me to be taken back?" Tongogara made no answer to this remark.

I said to Tongogara: "If that is so why was I taken? I was not a member of the Security Forces and was growing fruit and vegetables for black and white alike."

"Yes, you were farming close to the border; but you did nothing to help the comrades. If you had you would have been left alone. There are many whites helping us and they are not harmed," he finished coolly. (I was to hear this again from other commanders.)

I definitely got the impression that our capture alive had been a mistake made by local commanders but that their leaders had had to support them after the event. After this exchange our escort squeezed on board and we set off with Patrick still in front and with another commander, Kenneth, in the seat vacated by the woman. We still had about another 150 kilometres to go to reach Tembwe in the north, not far from the Zambian border. We reached the Tembwe camp at about one p.m. and, after sitting in the stationary vehicle for some time with the perspiration pouring from us, we set off walking into the bush once more.

On arrival at our new bivouac area we were surprised to see that we were to have a new tent; apparently because the rains were expected soon. The tent was pitched about five kilometres from Tembwe camp from where we were supplied. However, the next day we again moved for a short distance crossing a wide river bed which was almost dry. Here the tent was re-erected and the guerrillas who had accompanied us on the long journey were relieved by a platoon of fresh guards. They were under the command of one Trevor, an ex-night-club barman from Salisbury. Enoch, the medical orderly, was also replaced by another orderly, Comrade Africa. We grew to like both these individuals. Both Africa and

Trevor spoke good English and were agreeable types. They did their best to make our stay more pleasant than the previous weeks and months had been and the food improved appreciably. We asked ourselves if we were being softened up for something.

We now had a new logistics junior commander who called himself 'Captain'. We had left Killer behind at the caves and were not heartbroken at not having him, Lamec, and MacDonald with us. Seduce was still with us. Before joining the guerrillas Seduce had been a school teacher in the Salisbury area. He was quite an intelligent man and often asked for information about life in England. He sometimes asked questions about the British political parties, why there was an election every four or five years, how a government in power could be defeated by a vote in the House of Commons, and so on. He also asked about the role of an opposition party and the purpose of the House of Lords. After escorting us to our present area Seduce had left to rejoin them. Captain was also quite fluent in English and so were many of our new guards. They were a friendly and helpful lot but always very vigilant about guarding us. However, sometimes the heat of the day became too much for them and one or two would doze. Captain used to prowl around and if he could manage to take a weapon away from a sleeping sentry he would be reported to Commander Trevor. Punishment was physical and immediate. In most armies there are many forms of punishment, stoppage of pay or leave, and withdrawal of privileges and so on, before one comes to the court-martial stage. With ZANLA this was not possible. They had no pay, no leave and no privileges, and courts martial were out of the question. They had scales of physical punishment: I only saw them beaten on the buttocks whilst they lay face down on the ground. For offences like having their weapons taken from them whilst sleeping they usually received twenty cuts administered by the local commander with a stick cut from the bush. It was soon over and forgotten, for apparently no records were kept of this punishment. Generally speaking discipline was of a high standard and I was always impressed with the comradeship at all levels. Throughout my enforced stay with them I did not see or hear any quarrelling or fighting among them but did witness many examples of self-sacrifice one to another.

Much to my surprise ZANLA had specific codes of behaviour and all ranks were taught these. At one time I came across them printed in the *Zimbabwe News* and copied them out.

> All officers and comrades of our army must
> improve their military art, march forward
> and courageously towards certain victory
> in the war and resolutely, thoroughly,
> wholly and completely wipe out the enemy.
> We must heighten our sense of discipline
> and resolutely carry out orders, carry out
> policy, carry out the three rules of
> discipline and nine points of attention.
> Our army's three main rules of discipline
> and nine points of attention have been
> practised for many years. As to other
> matters that need attention, the lead-
> ership in different areas must lay down
> additional points in accordance with specific
> conditions and orders of their enforcement.
> Three main rules of discipline and nine
> points of attention are as follows:
> 1. Obey all orders in all your actions.
> 2. Do not take a single needle or piece
>   of thread from the masses.

3. Turn in everything captured.

The nine points of attention:

1. Speak politely.
2. Pay fairly for what you buy.
3. Return everything you borrow.
4. Pay for everything you damage.
5. Do not hit or swear at people.
6. Do not take liberty with them.
7. Do not damage crops.
8. Do not take liberty with women.
9. Do not ill-treat captives.

Obviously these rules were not always observed.

Like so many others we had met, Captain led a double life; that is to say, officially he was logistics man but he was also engaged in gathering intelligence. There always seemed to be one among the guards who was under instructions to make friends with us and listen to our conversation. Sometimes they would spend hours talking to Jon Kennerly about pop singers and the latest records or would discuss religion with Johannes Maartens. At other times they would lie close to us and pretend to be asleep. We were all aware of their real purpose and thought we recognised them all. However, who can know for sure?

At this time and in spite of our improved conditions we were all becoming depressed at our hopeless situation. We had received not one message or letter from any interested or disinterested person and as far as we knew no one at home knew we were still alive. In desperation I decided to write a letter to Robert Mugabe asking for an early release because of our mental and physical condition and, failing that, to be given the right to contact the British Consul in Maputo and the International Red Cross. After several drafts we agreed on one for I wanted all four of us to sign the letter. I wrote out the letter secretly and tucked it away in my makeshift pillow together with other hidden papers. These consisted of some notes I had been keeping up to date in a small school note book given to me by Jon (he had given up the Shona lessons for which he was given the book) a letter to Jennifer and some poetry I had written. These papers were all concealed in a wollen pullover inside a small plastic-coated sack which served as my pillow. Obviously the letter to the ZANU President and the letter to Jennifer were not of any use in the pillow but we could not risk giving them to a junior commander and hoped to persuade a senior commander to take them when the opportunity offered. I tried to do this writing in secret but it was well nigh impossible when we were so closely watched. We did not even have the protection of a latrine to screen us from prying eyes. I must have been seen writing on more than one occasion and so I let it be known that I was keeping notes for a book I would write and that I had the 'blessing' of Commander Tongogara. (He had in fact asked sarcastically at one time if I would write a book if and when I was released).

One morning just after 8 a.m. we were told that we were to go to the river and wash our clothes. This was most unusual for since we had arrived at this place our clothes had to be washed when we went for a bath in the evening. We set off and spent some two hours at the river much longer than was necessary to wash the few clothes that we had. I suspected that something was afoot and when we returned to the tent I had a good look round to see if anything had been disturbed or was missing from my bed. Nothing seemed to have been disturbed and my 'secret' papers were still in the pillow. However, I had had a few cigarettes in my jacket pocket and they were so few in number that I was able to know that two had been taken. I was sure that the cigarettes were not the cause of the visit as we had always found the guerrillas very honest. Someone had searched the tent and on the spur of the moment could not resist taking the two cigarettes.

The next morning just after first light Commander Trevor entered the tent accompanied by Comrade Africa, the medical orderly, and a Comrade Basher who was a junior commander and responsible for the guards. The absence of Captain was significant. He had probably searched the tent the previous morning. We were informed that they had come to conduct a search of all our belongings. I realised that they knew already what they were looking for and so I went to my pillow and gave them the papers. Trevor showed no surprise but went through the routine of searching the belongings of all four of us.

After they had left I was summoned to Trevor's shelter and was asked to explain what I had been doing. We went through all the papers and notes together. The two letters were self-explanatory but the notes worried him as, stupidly, I had written some criticism of my interrogation and had also mentioned my beating in Rhodesia with the baggage strap. Trevor told me that all the papers would have to go to High Command and a decision made there as to the action to be taken. He himself was of the opinion that I might get them back. Meanwhile he would also confiscate the pen and unused paper. Some weeks later I was informed that the letter to Robert Mugabe had been delivered. I never did get the notes back although I was often told that they were coming back. I once asked Josiah Tungamirai to get them back for me and he said he would. He had seen them and thought them not dangerous to ZANLA. The letter to Jennifer was never delivered. Sometime later, after repeated requests, the pen and the blank paper were returned to me and I again started to write notes on the daily happenings. I now did this openly and it was never objected to but they were sometimes asked for and read. I kept the notes simple and without criticism. These I brought back with me and used them as an 'aide mémoire' for this book.

The lack of exercise was worrying us all. Our guard commanders never liked us to exercise in case we were seen by the masses; and I suspect that they also thought we might be in training for an escape attempt. Also it made their tasks of guarding us more difficult. During my short time in the little grass hut I had persuaded the guard commander, Weber, to let me walk a circular course round the hut. He would only let me walk a course of about fifty paces with guards standing in the middle of the circuit. I was in danger of catching myself up on this short walk and suffering the fate of the Oozlum bird. By dint of going the 'wrong' side of the trees I managed to extend it to about a hundred paces but soon we moved, switching yet again from complete inactivity to long forced marches. In our new location Johannes complained, protesting that walking was his *muti* (medicine) and between us we persuaded Trevor to let us walk a course of about two hundred paces, accompanied by guards. We attempted to do this 25 times a day but often could not because of 'runny tummies' and then our only exercise came in frequent trips with the *badza*. Flies continued to bother us here and they seemed to follow a pattern. There were four phases. In the morning there were many of the ordinary house flies; in the afternoon we suffered from the large noisy tsetse flies (there were no cattle in this area because of these). One afternoon Jon Kennerly killed 123 tsetse flies in the tent. These were followed in the early evening by the small irritating mopani flies and at night—all night—the mosquitoes pestered us. At this time we were being given two anti-malarial tablets per week and in addition persuaded Trevor to obtain for us a tin of insect-repellent spray. The mopani flies nested in the trunks of trees and we were astonished to find that they made a honey which the guerrillas collected and ate.

Naturally we often considered the chances of making an escape bid. After the Second World War I had read many books by successful and unsuccessful escapers but our conditions were somewhat different. Apart from being very closely guarded, we were never fit and practically no movement was permitted. The greatest handicap was the colour of our skin. There appeared to be no whites in Mozambique outside the large towns and all the inhabitants, particularly in the rural areas, were hostile to and suspicious of whites. Between us and the Rhodesian border the countryside was full of guerrillas living in the bush and the terrain was so rugged as to make silent movement during the hours of darkness was almost impossible. There was also the problem of obtaining food and water.

As usual we were camped in a saucer-like valley. In addition to our close ring of guards the ridges surrounding us were manned by guerrillas. Both groups closed in during the hours of darkness. We were told that the outer ring was to keep the masses away and that they would attack us if they knew we were there. It was hardly likely that there were any 'masses' in the sort of wild areas in which we were kept but certainly they did not want us to be seen by anyone other than the guards and the commanders in case our location was leaked to the Rhodesian Security Forces. They were nervous of informers, and particularly of the Selous Scouts and there was also talk of an anti-Frelimo terrorist group operating in the area.

We were in this area for about 28 days. We now had

more time to consider our plight and could see no hope for our release, for we had been told that we were unlikely to be released before the Patriotic Front had won the war and that we would then be taken back with them. We had no reading matter, except for old copies of the *Zimbabwe News* and still no indoor games. We did find the old copies of the *Zimbabwe News* interesting to read and we were, I think, quite untouched by the propaganda contained in them. All of us had had first-hand knowledge or experience of incidents, ambushes and attacks in Rhodesia during the past three years and it was amusing to read the exaggerated reports of them. Jim Black had been a police reservist in Melsetter and was astounded to read of the large number of casualties and damage inflicted in that area of which he was unaware! Again, the reports of the attacks on Umtali were quite ridiculous; but no doubt the guerrillas believed it all and it boosted their morale. Some of the guerrillas had a few books and these turned out to be the works of Karl Marx or Engels: not what we wanted for we were in need of light escapist reading and certainly we were not interested in Communist literature. We often had visits from commanders who were based in the nearby Tembwe camp but they were relatively junior and were merely inquisitive and not helpful.

We were now the responsibility of Commander Kenneth who was of higher rank than Trevor and was in charge of a very large area. Trevor remained in command of our bivouac area under the orders of Kenneth who visited us about once a week. He was a strange man, obviously devoted to the cause of ZANU. He was patient with us and our many requests but nothing much came of them. Our health improved, apart from the persistent stomach upsets, and as we were now permitted to strip to the waist, the horrible rash I had developed on my chest and shoulders disappeared. This rash had troubled me for some time and was due to spending all day in sweat-soaked and dirty clothes. At one time I asked Jon Kennerley to cut off the hair on my chest and shoulders with an old pair of scissors. It was a very painful operation but I was grateful to him. Jon Kennerly had also been troubled, with his back being covered in pus-filled spots, but from now on his condition improved.

My trousers were by now bare at the backside and there was no material available to patch them. When I acquired another pair of trousers I decided to cut the worn pair into shorts and used the material from the lower legs to patch the holes. This I did successfully and still have the shorts as a souvenir to 'show off'. I had never been any good at domestic tasks like this before but perhaps I had hidden talents. Shorts were a boon and Jim Black was lucky enough to have retained a stout pair he was wearing at his capture. Jon Kennerly made himself a pair from a small—too small really—piece of denim cloth. They were more like a bikini than shorts and some of the women guerrillas were quite embarrassed. Even the male guerrillas used to express their disapproval but never forbade them. On the move and during the visits of senior commanders we had to dress fully. Johannes Maartens had no shorts but sometimes would lie around in his underpants, worn grey over the months, a sight for sore eyes. Washing our pants and socks in cold dirty water was always a problem, but I sometimes used a tin to boil them over the fire. The guerrilla Tokyo, an ex-houseboy, was appalled at my boiling my socks and so he offered to wash my clothes when he did his own. He was as strong as a horse though small in stature and of odd appearance with a cast in one eye. A great character, he performed many kindnesses for us all during the time he was with us; he was always offering to mend our clothes and repair our split boots. A tremendous worker, when on cook-house duty he did the work of three men and looked after us well. He was very clever with his hands and could make a new pair of uppers for boots out of animal skins, entirely without tools except for a razor blade and needle. His official role was machine-gunner and was no doubt good at that too, but he was a domestic at heart. I regret I was unable to thank him and say goodbye when we left on another panic move but he was confined to his blankets with malaria some distance away. I would like to meet him again.

We were still in the area about 150 kilometres north west of Tete and about five kilometres from the Tembwe camp. However, we were on the wrong side of the large river which was between us and the main camp and when the rains came this would present a problem. We were told that the rains in the area were very heavy and flooding was frequent. One Saturday afternoon we saw unusual activity in our area and a certain amount of packing was going on. However, we were told nothing and our tent remained untouched. We had noticed that two junior commanders had arrived from the main camp and we guessed that they had brought orders for a move. The date was 4 November. Sure enough, just before last light we were told to clear the tent and pack. The tent was struck and a quick meal was served.

8

Just after dark we set off in file to walk to the main camp. Crossing the riverbed was quite hazardous in the dark for there was about half a kilometre of slippery rocks to clamber over. When we reached the outskirts of the main camp we were ordered aboard an ambulance vehicle together with Commander Trevor and three guards. Once again we were very cramped but glad of the ride. The remainder of the guerrillas with baggage and rations were to be taken by lorry to our new destination. Not long after leaving we stopped at a ration and fuel dump. After refuelling the vehicle we took on board a case of *Sumovit* orange squash and set off once more. I remember that just before we moved off a very pretty girl opened the doors of the ambulance and after saying "Hello" added "Good Luck". I at least appreciated this for she might have risked a reprimand.

We travelled all night at a moderate speed and reached a camp outside Tete at about seven a.m. After dismounting we walked some distance into the bush away from the camp and established ourselves near a dry riverbed. The tent was erected but after one day we asked for it to be moved for it was in full sun and very hot indeed. This was done and later grass beds were built for the four of us. In addition a bathing shelter was built, for apparently Captain, who was still with us, was to be assisted by a women guerrilla. We were not to use the river for bathing because the masses went there: water would be brought to us for the daily wash-down. Our new area began to assume an air of permanence when another tent was erected as headquarters for the commander, shelters were built for the cook-house and also for the nearest guards. The guerrillas were encouraged to build shelters and beds for themselves as the rains were expected daily. We were amused by Johannes Maartens who every morning for the past three weeks had cast his experienced farmer's eyes to the skies and forecast imminent rain. Inevitably when it did come some weeks later he said: "I told you so," as if it had not rained at this time of the year from time immemorial. Even so we were caught out, for the tent leaked like a sieve and the water rushed over its floor from the higher slopes. Even the usual trench round the outside of the tent could not take it. However, a lorry tarpaulin was put over the tent and we eventually managed to keep the water out.

After the first rain a fantastic change took place in the appearance of the surrounding bush which earlier had been burnt thoroughly. Trees which had looked dead and petrified came out in glorious leaf and the grass grew apace. Very soon the burnt 'desert' which was always so depressing to look at became a green jungle and sprang into life. Hundreds of wild flowers, including many varieties of lilies, bloomed within days of the rain. There were many wild hibiscus bushes, some of which appeared to have flowers of differing colours on the same bush. Birds had never been plentiful in the burnt bush apart from parakeets and the trumpeter hornbill which made a noise like a child crying; now there were birds of wonderful hue in abundance. Beautiful lizards emerged from the rocky outcrops in attractive colour-designs. Some of them were quite big and these were killed and eaten by the guerrillas as a delicacy. Of the four of us only Jon Kennerly would eat the meat of these when it was offered. Some of the insects were also highly coloured and I remember some bright-red beetles emerging from a hole in the ground looking as if they were garbed in red velvet. I also remember how, one afternoon after a rainstorm, we watched fascinated as over thirty 'baby' chameleons emerged from the ground. They were delicate-looking reptiles and as they appeared we put them on differently coloured foilage to observe them changing colour. The following day they had all disappeared except for one we found which had almost doubled in size. We were still troubled by snakes and also at this time by tree rats. With the rain the mosquitoes were more numerous than ever before, and after dark we would also see hundreds of fireflies emerging from the ground. When they entered the dark tent they gave quite a lot of illumination. We were experiencing violent rain storms and many trees were collapsing. An enormous tree over our tent looked very unsafe but we were reassured by the number of tree rats still in occupation in the diseased trunk. No doubt, like the rats on a sinking ship, they would know when to leave.

It was whilst we were here that we received combs, toothbrushes and toothpaste. We also received articles of clothing such as shirts and trousers. These were all second-hand but had been freshly laundered. They were obviously donated from abroad for refugees, for one day when two sacks of clothing were brought in and emptied we were amused to see the reaction of the guerrillas. The clothes were women's jackets and coats for a cold climate, trimmed with fur. Presumably they came from Scandinavia. However, they were distributed among our guards and within days the fur had been removed and the coats and jackets altered to serve a purpose. These guerrillas were indeed very good at 'make and mend' with the minimum of tools. They used thread from plastic-covered sacks and often the bivouac area resembled a sewing bee. They had to be good at alterations as at this time in Mozambique they were entirely dependent on handouts, mostly from overseas. Sometimes alterations were beyond their skills and I well remember walking behind one of the guerrillas who was doubled over as he walked. I recognised him and did not remember him as being handicapped in any way. He appeared to be in some discomfort and then I noticed that the trousers he wore, a pair of riding slacks buttoning up the sides, looked as if they had previously belonged to a teenage girl. The poor fellow, who was quite well endowed physically, was in some pain for the slacks were altogether too tight between his legs.

During my captivity I often asked the guerrillas why they had joined ZANLA, leaving their homes and in many cases profitable employment. Some had become guerrillas because they were bored or unemployed but most had joined because of the inequality of their life in Rhodesia. Many had complained about unfair treatment from the police. One commander told me that he had been doing well in Salisbury with a number of employees taking tricycles containing cakes, cigarettes and sweets round the industrial sites during the tea breaks and at lunch time. After much trouble he had obtained all the right pieces of paper, licences and so on, and his business had been fully legitimate. However, the white shopkeepers had complained to the authorities about the competition and his employees had been continually harassed by the police and had left him. Another told me that he had been a barman in a night club and in addition had had his own business which was run by his father. They were comfortably off financially. One evening two white soldiers left the bar rather the worse for drink. He followed them to the door to watch their progress. Outside the bar the two soldiers stopped a black youth to ask him for a light. Apparently a non-smoker, he did not have any matches or a lighter. Thereupon the soldiers beat him up. A police van appeared on the scene with two white constables in the front. The two soldiers walked away and without any questioning the black youth was flung into the back of the van and driven away. This was enough for the barman and the next day he left for Mozambique. (Of course the ex-barman could have been mistaken in the interpretation he put on this incident. I pointed out that the police may have been taking the 'beaten up' black for medical treatment. However, he did not think so.) Other sad tales of a similar nature abounded.

Whatever their original reasons for becoming guerrillas, after political indoctrination they were all fanatical supporters of the fight for majority rule and equal opportunity. They appeared to be well-informed politically and were kept up to date at lectures of political events throughout the world. They were avid readers of the *Zimbabwe News* and also listened to all the radio news they could. Some of them, even quite junior guerrillas, were much travelled, having been to Russia, China, or Rumania, or to East Germany. Most had been to Tanzania. They used to point out that in those countries they had been on equal terms with the whites and liked them very much. However, I gathered that Russia was the least popular country, although I never managed to ascertain why.

We were now getting much better food, with a tough, sinewy chicken once a week. We were always complaining about the complete lack of fresh meat but were getting some processed tinned beef and even some tomato purée from Romania. The purée was made into delicious soup by Jim Black who used to crouch over the pot like one of the witches in Macbeth. As he added dried milk, margarine (when we had any) and also brown sugar I am sure he muttered incantations in Swahili. This tomato soup was a real treat and we had to watch its progress from the fire to our mugs or it decreased in quantity on the way.

One day a large billy goat about the size of a Shetland pony was bought for us. We were told it had cost a fortune and was meant to meet our demand for fresh meat. It looked very old and tough and I suggested it be kept for a time on the new grass to sweeten it a bit. However, it escaped by dragging its 'anchor' and thus sealed its fate for it was immediately killed on recapture. The meat was very tough and strong tasting and none of us enjoyed it, not even Johannes. Whilst in the bush I saw them attempt to shoot guinea fowl and buck for the pot many times but they never hit their target once. One large buck was killed with a bayonet after being lamed by a stone thrown at its legs. Their marksmanship was definitely of a low standard and this was well known throughout Rhodesia. From what I could observe the standard of the maintenance of their weapons was not good and I did not once see a commander inspect their weapons. Often I noticed the inside of a muzzle of an AK 47 or SAR full of soil where the muzzle had been pressed into the ground.

(I suppose this accounted for the large number of 'terrorist' casualties claimed in our communiqués, for such statistics are hardly in the tradition of guerrilla warfare. I remember that in the Malaya campaign in the fifties it was a cause for celebration if four or five communist terrorists were killed in one day. Every terrorist casualty, dead or captured, had to be identified by the police from their Rogues Gallery records before he could be 'claimed' by the army as a 'kill'. This presented difficulties for the contact could occur deep in the jungle far from any police or army H.Q. and in the early days the bodies had to be carried out. Sometimes this took several days and in that climate corpses disintegrated very quickly. Another problem was that a patrol carrying a corpse or corpses was very vulnerable to a communist terrorist ambush. As a result, after a time only the head of the dead man (or woman) was brough back for identification. Later patrols were issued with a camera and the casualty was photographed propped against a tree and then buried).

Once again we organised a walking circle but I had recurring trouble with my left knee and ankle. I was later informed by the medical authorities in Pretoria that this was probably due to malnutrition. I was eating very little though I did manage the rice, mixing it with brown sugar, and Comrade Africa was liberal with vitamin A and C tablets as well as multivitamins. I am sure these kept me going, although my arms and legs were like sticks. We still had the ancient transistor set but eventually were reduced to listening to the news only, after which the batteries were removed and placed in the sun in the hope that they would be rejuvenated. We were about thirty miles from Tete and we were informed that there were no batteries available there. This restriction of radio listening suited me fine for so much rubbish was broadcast. My personal preference was for classical music but there was little of that and the set was not really good enough. Some of the afternoon programmes were absolute drivel and I remember how the tent used to empty when a serial version of *This side of Innocence* by Taylor Caldwell was broadcast. However, there had been no question of switching off for Johannes used to like the programme and another serial about a farming family. These and the religious services had been

132

allocated to him as his choice. The biggest blow about not being able to listen to the radio was that we had been hoping for messages via the request programmes. Both Johannes and I had mentioned this in our letters but of course we did not know if they had ever got through. Anyway we never received a message and as the radio was not working for much of the time that was not surprising. Another thing that irritated us all was the absurd chatter of disc jockeys who had nothing to say. This was particularly apparent in the early morning programme. Nevertheless I felt sorry for the individual who had to earn his living this way. We were also keenly aware that quite often the news from Salisbury made no mention of Rhodesia but seemed concerned with the troubles of other countries. Apparently all was peace and harmony in Rhodesia.

One Sunday afternoon we were told to get properly dressed and 'at once'. The usual large group presently approached escorting a very high-level group of commanders. There were Tongogara, Josiah Tungamirai and his senior, the Chief Political Commissar Mey Hurimbo, Joshua Misihairambwi (whose appointment I cannot remember)—and many others. We were each given a bottle of beer (they called these 'little brown bottles', and I certainly thought them too small) and later a meal of meat and *sadza* was served to us all. Everyone was quite cheerful and Tongogara was in good form. He talked of his friend Ian Smith and told me the following story: At one of the early 'Settlement' talks both he and Ian Smith were at a cocktail party. Ian Smith was asked by one of the others present whether he had met Tongogara. Smith replied that he did not know, for they all had black faces and large flat noses, and he could not tell one from the other. I do not know if there is any truth in this story but certainly Tongogara roared with laughter when he told it. He claimed to have known Ian Smith for years and said his mother had known Ian Smith's mother. He told us he bore Smith no grudge for he was looking after his own white people; and similarly Robert Mugabe was looking after the interests of the black man. He added, however, that if the rate of white emigration continued at its present level the white minority would soon consist of Ian and Janet Smith! It was an interesting fact that many of the guerrillas were very concerned when the news was announced on the radio that increasing numbers of whites were leaving Rhodesia. They would say: "Why are they leaving? We want them to stay. We are all Zimbabweans. Look at all the whites that are in the government of Mozambique. I used to point out that the reasons they were leaving were pretty obvious and that I wished I had had the sense to leave before they captured me. I tried to tie Tongogara down to telling us when we would be released but he evaded that sort of question. He did admit however that he was getting tired of having to visit us whenever he was in our area. I asked him how it was he appeared to know when the air raids were coming, and had everyone on the move away from the camps, sometimes days ahead of the attacking aircraft, sometimes hours. He was a bit taken aback at this question but "I feel it here" he said and rubbed his stomach.

I mentioned that I had read in the *Zimbabwe News* that he had stated he was not a communist. He replied: "I am not a communist but we accept aid from any source that will help us in our struggle. After all Churchill did the same in the Second World War. Britain and America refused to give us arms." He continued: "Why do they go on fighting when they cannot win?" He spoke more in sorrow than in anger.

After they had left we were certainly more cheerful

as a result of their visit and held an inquest on everything that had been said. We agreed that there was reason for some optimism and that perhaps our release was in sight. (Wishful thinking again.) It was now early December and we began to think: "Perhaps we'll be home for Christmas". We could certainly do with some cheering up for the four of us were too much in each other's pockets, together 24 hours a day. We were tired of hearing each other's stories and sometimes did not say a word for hours on end. We were losing the ability to converse and also becoming easily irritated with each other. Jon Kennerly sometimes was moody and silent for days, refusing all food. When he got over it he would often seek the company of the young guards with whom, age-wise, he had much more in common. They liked Jon very much and hated to see him sullen and depressed. He was always interested in uniforms, weapons and the history of the regiments of the British Army and I would talk to him at length on such matters. He would tell me that when he was free he would go to Britain and join the British Army and he would be full of questions as to the method of doing so. I had much sympathy for him and tried to amuse him with humorous stories and verse.

I remember once discussing with him the importance of discipline and during the course of the discussion told him the following true story: "During the Second World War I was attached to one of the units of the American Forces which arrived in Northern Ireland. The difference in the standard of discipline btween the British and American forces was most marked and commanders of the U.S. units were instructed by their General to improve matters quickly. Three or four weeks later whilst attending a conference of officers at an American H.Q., the door burst open and a G.I. put his head round the door and shouted to the senior officer present: 'I am taking your jeep, Colonel!' and then withdrew, slamming the door. To my astonishment the colonel was looking quite pleased with this and said: 'There you are gentlemen, that's what I meant by the marked improvement in our discipline. Two weeks ago he wouldn't even have told me.' "

Another anecdote which amused him was as follows: For the Crossing of the Rhine operation in March 1945 my Regiment was with the 15th Scottish Division. After the successful crossing all troops were addressed by the Divisional Commander to be congratulated on the part they had played and also to be briefed as to the correct attitude to be adopted towards the German civilian population. The 'order of the day' was non-fraternisation. When the General had finished his address he asked if there were any questions. A Jock at the back of the crowd clustered round the General's jeep complained that he did not know what was meant by non-fraternisation. The General thought for a few seconds and knowing what was uppermost in the mind of the soldier said: "Non-fraternisation means that you may sleep with a German girl if you are invited but you must on no account stay for breakfast."

I tried to amuse him with these stories but there were many times when he irritated us all. There was no doubt, however, we all did that to each other and I grew very fond of him. He had been a prisoner for the longest time and was very young but he came out of it very well. Ruda, a girl guerrilla, used to try and make a friend of Jon. Officially she was in logistics but we suspected that she was also engaged in intelligence duties. Jon Kennerly was very keen to get hold of a black beret and a pair of knee-length black boots (Cuban or Russian). These boots had just been issued to our guards and had the effect of making them almost immobile. Ruda promised to get him both but later found she could not and Jon was furious. He refused even to talk to her, but later when we finally moved from that area she got her revenge by taking back a green drill-suit he had.

We prisoners also argued: one day a slanging match took place between Jon Kennerly and Jim Black. Voices were raised and bad language used. The guerrillas were more than interested. That night after dark we received a visit from Commander Trevor accompanied by medical orderly Africa who was to act as interpreter. Trevor was younger than three of us but managed to give a fatherly talk on the theme that we were all comrades together and should practice tolerance towards each other, seeing the difficult position we were in. He asked us all to speak frankly to him of our problems with one another and observed that it could be difficult for us and for him if we openly quarrelled. It was very well done and was just what was required. It healed the breach for a time.

Johannes Maartens had good days and bad but generally speaking kept very well. From his accounts he was now as fit as he had ever been since his major operation in Groote Schuur hospital. Africa, the medical orderly, was very conscientious and took great pains over Johannes' treatment. In addition he was always studying medical books. It always seemed to me that Africa would have made a good doctor if he had had the opportunity. Nothing was ever too much trouble for him, not only for the white prisoners but for the guerrillas who yelled constantly for his services. He was quite intelligent and always very calm.

(One of the things I found most irritating after my release was that no one I spoke to in Rhodesia was prepared to believe that some of the guerrillas were kind and helpful. They were all 'baddies' beyond redemption. I remember one white hostess chiding me for the praise I

gave to the medical orderly who looked after Johannes
Maartens so well—and, come to think of it, was concerned about the health of us all. She was very proud of her
long-serving black domestic staff who without exception
were paragons of all the virtues. I asked her what would
be her opinion of them if she came from her bedroom one
morning to discover that they had gone across the
border to join the 'terrs'. Would they suddenly become
evil, cruel men? She said she could not imagine them doing such a thing but had to agree it had happened to
many other employers. I think she got the point. During
my life I have always been able to see and appreciate the
other fellow's point of view. In war this can be a severe
handicap: I often used to ask myself what I would be doing if I had been born black in Rhodesia or South Africa!
Certainly during my years in these two countries I had
seen the urgent need for change in the status of the black
man. I agreed with their aspirations but disagreed with
their methods of bringing about change by violent
means. However, they claimed their patience was exhausted).

Johannes loved playing draughts and at this time we
made our own board out of cardboard using bottle caps
as counters. Jon and I soon got tired of the game for we
were always being beaten but Johannes and Jim Black
used to play for hours. They used to hold inquests after
very game and for some reason I found this intensely irritating. It all seemed too trivial and yet it was obviously
better than doing nothing.

We were all jealous of Jim Black for his capture
would not, apparently, affect him financially. He was a
forester in government service and at the end of each
month would inform us smugly of his accrued pay and
leave entitlement. Jon Kennerly also expected that his
pay would be placed to his credit but did not expect it to

amount to much. Both Johannes Maartens and myself were self-employed farmers and our businesses would not function in our absence but losses would mount with every passing day we spent as prisoners!

About this time we were given some old newspapers and this was exactly what we wanted. Most were in English and had come from Zambia or Tanzania. However, there were some copies of the *Herald*, the major Rhodesian daily, about six weeks old, and these gave us the details of the first Viscount disaster and the mortar attack on Umtali. I was keen to read the details of the Umtali attack for I thought that Jennifer was there at the time and hearing of the attack on the radio earlier I had worried about the possibility of her being a casualty. The report reassured me. We were told that the newspapers were to be treated with care and were to be returned. After reading through them two or three times over we replenished our toilet-paper stocks and repacked the papers. They were very 'tatty' by this time and fit only for toilet paper.

In our present position we could hear trains, and judging by the whistling there must be a level-crossing close by. Sometimes the trains sounded like helicopters and we would think there was a raid in the offing. Another sound we had not heard for a long time was the constant drumming that went on from a nearby Mozambique village. On Saturday nights the local inhabitants were very restless for the drumming increased in intensity and duration. No doubt the masses were being summoned to the Saturday night 'hop'.

We were all dreaming dreams and sometimes experienceing nightmares although I do not remember Jim Black ever confessing to having had a dream. Johannes would ask each morning to be told of our dreams and he would interpret them. He had a theory that a dream should be turned 'upside down' to get at the true meaning but I noticed he only did that to the unpleasant ones or those that were gloomy. I remember that one morning he seemed more than usually depressed and he told me of a dream he had had in which he had been released and returned home to find that he was not welcome! I reminded him of his belief that dreams should be reversed and that this would make it into a pleasant one. He agreed and brightened up at this. One dream I had which was popular with all of us was as follows: the four of us found ourselves, free, in Cecil Square in Salisbury. We decided to have a drink together before going our separate ways. We were in the bar doing just that when we heard singing and shouting from many people outside the Meikles Hotel where we were. We looked through the window and observed hundreds of people, black, white and coloured, dancing together whilst some were singing and others were crying. I went out to enquire what it was all about, thinking that surely all these people could not be celebrating our release. I was told that a ceasefire had been announced and everyone was celebrating this. I thought that this was how it should be and could be if it were not for the politicians and so-called leaders lusting for power. Johannes made no suggestion that this dream should be reversed.

One day a Commander Grainger came to our 'camp' and stayed for three or four days. He was reported to be a very experienced operations commander and whilst he was in the area made a point of spending much time with us. He claimed to have brought with him eleven prisoners, who had surrendered after an ambush on the Rhodesian Security Forces. We were unable to verify this and certainly saw no prisoners; but if they had been black soldiers we would not have seen them. They were always kept well away from us although we had caught glimpses of them on the move during the air raids. We found Grainger quite agreeable and we wondered why he was with us. I thought there were two possibilities. Either he was relieving Commander Trevor or (wishful thinking) he had come to escort us back across the border into Rhodesia for subsequent release. This would be the easiest way of unloading us without documentation at borders or intervention of Frelimo. I hinted to him that that was what he was meant to do but he neither denied nor confirmed this theory. He only said that he was with us awaiting fresh orders. However, one morning we awoke to find him gone. I am still convinced that our release in that way had been considered but that Frelimo having begun to show an interest in us it was too late for ZANLA to act without their agreement. About this time also the Frelimo military camp at Tete was heavily attacked by the Rhodesian Air Force and a great deal of damage and many casualties resulted. We heard the bombs exploding and knew that that would set our release back a bit. There was much Frelimo activity round our camp and we were told that Frelimo were looking for Rhodesian ground forces. Our walks were stopped: we were confined to the immediate area of our tent and compelled to keep under cover.

Our personal possessions and food stocks were now on the increase. When the *sadza*, or macaroni or rice, was delivered it was now possible for us to have an alternative 'relish' from a tin. On one memorable day we even shared a tin of pineapple chunks and sometimes we got fresh mangoes. We began to acquire personal 'hoards' of leftovers and produced them at mealtimes like old ladies in a boarding house. We were also issued with more toilet soap—Cussons Imperial Leather— no less! Things were decidedly looking up. We were still very depressed, however, and at this time particularly Jon Kennerly; and there was little conversation between the four of us. I was sick of the sight of naked male bodies and the smell of sweat. Johannes had bouts of false cheerfulness and would suddenly say: "What shall we talk about?" Nobody bothered to reply. My eyesight was now giving me trouble, always in the late afternoon and evening. I seemed to have a film over my eyes and they were constantly weeping. It certainly was not from reading too much! Africa, the medical orderly, prescribed Vitamin A tablets but they seemed to have no effect whatsoever. I suspected that it was due to some particular blossom on the trees over us and certainly I had no more trouble when I left that area.

9

Many times in captivity I tried to draw up a personal balance sheet of my situation. My liabilities ran into pages and my assets were dubious and negligible. I tried to convince myself that the complete abstinence from alcohol and my severely rationed pipe smoking must be good for me. I had lost much weight—too much— and in any case I had never been fat. I worried a great deal about Jennifer for I had left her many problems. Later I was to learn that our friends and neighbours had rallied to her assistance and she had coped very well. However, our farm had been occupied by the 'military' and no one ever advised her about getting any agreement or rent for it. This was to cause us much trouble and financial loss.

In my notes dated 20 December I had recalled that it was Christmas week, and still no sign of our release. We had no radio, no tobacco, no exercise; and almost no hope. Had we been completely forgotton by everone?

However, that afternoon we were visited by Josiah Tungamirai with the usual large escort. This time he was accompanied by two dour civilians who when introduced turned out to be Mozambique Government officials. They were security men and looked the part. The senior one was short, fat and rather severe-looking. His companion was well-built and wore spectacles. He was supposed to be the English speaker but as we had found before in Mozambique the English was very limited. Then followed one of those frustrating interviews: after we were all seated in the tent the short fat one made a long speech in Portuguese which the interpreter translated into very few words. The gist of the translation was that the leaders of ZANU and the Mozambique Government had agreed that Frelimo would take over the four white prisoners and be responsible for them. Then followed questions put to each of us in turn regarding our employment, location and date of capture, our military commitments, training and so on. When they came to me and my military training I pointed out that I had had no training or service with the Rhodesian Forces. They accepted this and no further details were asked which, bearing in mind the time all the translation took, was just as well. To give some idea of the standard of English translation, Jim Black had great difficulty in explaining what a forester was and eventually was listed as a gardener! While all this was going on Josiah Tungamirai sat silent and looking very glum. The two security officials got up and said they were now leaving but would be back sometime. As they were going I asked Josiah to explain to me what all this meant. He merely replied that he would come back soon and explain. As can be imagined we discussed the afternoon's events and tried to estimate the possible outcome. The general opinion was that because of the recent air raid on the Frelimo barracks we were being taken over as some sort of reprisal, but perhaps we were going to Maputo. We hoped so.

In our discussions on possible escape attempts I had come to the conclusion that Maputo would offer more opportunities. We might be able to get to the British Consulate, there would be ships in the harbour and we might get assistance from Portuguese whites. Another advantage would be that the colour of our skin would arouse less suspicion and hostility.

The next morning they all returned with even more guards and some guerrilla junior commanders. We were told to get ready to move at once and to leave everything behind except what we stood up in. We would not need blankets or spare clothes and were told not to take spare soap or food. I was determined to take my 'pillow-sack' which contained my jersey, spare slacks and my note book. In addition we had some clothing which had been washed that morning and was spread out to dry. This was gathered by one of the guards and stuffed into a cardboard box together with some biscuits. Surrounded by the guards we set off, walking very fast through the bush. Presently we came upon two Landrovers on a dirt road and the four of us got into the back with Commander Trevor; Josiah climbed into the front of the leading vehicle. The security officials and a Frelimo escort got into the second vehicle. Whilst we had been walking through the bush one of the guerrillas had whispered to me that we were on our way to Maputo.

I was dropping behind and some guerrillas behind me yelled "Move. Move". We caught up with the others when Josiah Tungamirai called a halt to get everyone together. I had my empty pipe in my mouth and Tungamirai remarked: "Ah, you are trying to look like Harold Wilson."

"On the contrary," I said. "I do not want to look like him. I would prefer to look like Margaret Thatcher."

Laughing, he said: "Surely she doesn't smoke a pipe."

Fatty, the Frelimo official, was looking blank at all this and questioned Tungamirai who explained the joke in Portuguese. Wilth some difficulty Farry managed to raise a faint smile but he still looked rather bewildered.

When we reached the tarmac road running north from Tete we in the front vehicle transferred to a more comfortable passenger-carrying vehicle belonging to ZANLA. Just outside Tete we turned down a road sign-posted 'To The Airfield'. We began to think again that it was just possible that we might be home for Christmas after all. According to our reckoning it was 21 December. (I have been asked how we kept track of days and dates without a calendar. We took some trouble over this by questioning each other each morning and when I was able to do so I entered dates into my notes. We often talked of making a calendar but never summoned up enough energy to do so.) Both vehicles stopped under an enormous wild fig tree short of the airfield and a conference between Josiah and the Mozambique government officials took place out of earshot. The Frelimo vehicle then moved off to the airfield while ours turned back and entered the airfield area by a little-used grass track. Here we were told to dismount and hide under some bushes.

Much to our disgust, Josiah drove off without a word; it surprised us, for he was normally a cheerful, talkative man who seemed to have some regard for us. (I remember that one afternoon when he visited us in a tent east of Tete he complained lightheartedly that we were costing ZANLA too much for our keep. I pointed out that any extras that were bought were also consumed by some of the guards and that in the recent past we had decided to economise, but having heard on the radio that Sweden had given ZANU about 800 000 dollars we had decided that economy was no longer necessary. Surely they could save money by releasing us! He thought this a great joke and laughed loud and long.)

We could see a fairly large aircraft standing alone on the runway and felt sure that we would soon travel on it. We got quite excited at the prospect but imagine our dismay when our aircraft started up, warmed up the engines and took off without us! Even Trevor and our guards seemed a little non-plussed and Jon got to his feet and waved his arms as the plane roared overhead proceeding south towards Maputo. This was a blow to our morale. However, we felt sure there would be another one, probably a special chartered flight.

Some time later the Frelimo Landrover returned and the security men told us that there had been a change of plan. They had brought us some rations as we would probably spend the rest of the day there. The rations, packed in a cardboard box, constituted food for one man for one day, probably emergency rations for an officer. Certainly we enjoyed them for the box contained a tin of bully beef, another of sardines, of apple juice, liquid chocolate, and a large packet of biscuits. What a pleasant surprise to find this sort of food in Mozambique. It was the only time we were to get rations like that.

That evening before dark our Frelimo guards were heavily reinforced until they stood in a circle around us about a metre apart from each other. After a meal of *sadza*, rice and meat, cooked Portuguese-style with garlic and spices, and all running with cooking oil, we were transported by Landrover to a place in the bush outside Tete but closer to the town than before. Here a tent had been erected and we were provided with pieces of plastic foam as mattresses. It was very hot and humid in the tent for we were in the Zambezi Valley and not far from the great river. Apart from ventilation 'windows' in the tent the roof was full of large holes and we wondered whether they had been caused by aircraft rockets or cannon. I did not sleep much as it was too hot and the mosquitoes were worse than ever. Trevor had been joined by another guerrilla commander whose freedom-fighting name was Alpha; they were to remain with us on liaison and interpreter duties until we took off from Tete. We had about thirty or more trigger-happy Frelimo soldiers as guards, none of whom spoke any English. Alpha, however, spoke English and Portuguese. The following morning I went outside the tent and started to walk towards some bushes to relieve myself and heard someone shout at me in a foreign tongue and the sound of a weapon being cocked. Trevor called out in English to 'stand still'. I did so and he angrily said we were not to move outside the tent without informing him so that he could obtain the permission of the Frelimo guard commander. So that was to be the pattern. Later I asked to go for a *badza* and was closely attended by four Frelimo soldiers throughout the operation. We spent that morning trying to seek some shade for it was excessively hot and sticky. Eventually we obtained permission to take our foam mattresses into a nearby copse but there the insect-life was almost unbearable. About three p.m. that afternoon Fatty and his companion arrived in a Landrover and told us to pack and get into the vehicle "Quick—quick", for the aircraft was waiting for us. We were ready in seconds and proceeded to the airfield. I was carrying my pillow sack, Jim Black the cardboard box, Johannes his heavy overcoat and Jon Kennerly a heavy bush coat he had hung on to for months. We arrived at the airfield and were left under guard in the porch of an uncompleted terminal building whilst Fatty and partner went off. Presently they returned and we were informed through Trevor that the aircraft could only take two. This was a serious blow. Trevor said that it was to be Johannes and myself and we perked up and picked up our belongings.

However, a Frelimo battalion commander who was present said emphatically "No"—that it must be the two younger ones. I felt close to tears and I am sure that Johannes felt the same. Jon Kennerly and Jim Black needed no further urging and, grabbing the cardboard box, Jim set off almost at a run. I called out to them to save us some cold beers. The cardboard box contained some clothing belonging to Johannes and myself, biscuits; and, more important, Johannes' soap and towel. It appeared that we had seen the last of those. I felt very sick. After all we had been through to get so close to flying to Maputo and then to be left behind. What sort of people were these Frelimo who arranged for you to board an aircraft and then found there were not enough seats?

The Frelimo battalion commander returned to us and beckoned to me and Johannes to get into the vehicle saying at the same time that we must not worry because we would take off the next morning at eight. Was this their morale boosting technique once again? Anyway I did not believe him but Johannes kept repeating to me that it would not be long until eight tomorrow: only one more night in that dreadful tent with the heat and the mosquitoes, and then we'd be in comparatively civilized Maputo with possibly a roof over our heads and a bed to sleep in. We set off back towards the site of the tent but Johannes asked if we could have a bath. We both thought we would be taken to the barracks for a shower but the commander said that it would have to be in the nearby Zambezi River. Had we got soap and towel? I had in my pillow case the small towel and the remains of my sugar issued months before and a tablet of soap. We were dropped at the approach to a long bridge which carried the main road over the river and with an escort of eight Frelimo soldiers walked down towards the water's edge. At the place where we had left the vehicle there was a main checkpoint at which all traffic had to have passes checked and vehicles searched. The Frelimo battalion commander told Trevor and Alpha not to hurry as he was taking the vehicle into Tete to arrange our flight for the morrow. We walked down to the river which was in flood. The dark brown water was rushing along at a terrific pace with floating trees and branches being carried along. However, there was a 'backwater' under the bridge where concrete blocks left behind by the builders formed a barrier which diverted the swirling waters. Here were dozens of Frelimo soldiers bathing in the small calm area. They were almost touching each other in the confined space. Apparently the water supplies in their camp had been cut off by the air raid and they had to use the river. Once again I wished we had asked for a bucket of clean water back in the tent for I could see that all the bathers had thick tide-marks of mud round their bodies. However, with some reluctance, I joined Johannes and we forced our way into the press of bodies, followed by Trevor and Alpha. My small towel and sugar sack had to do for the four of us. We were the objects of much attention and discussion by the black Frelimo soldiers and I was glad to get out and get dressed. All this time we were under guard from the bank. When we had finished Trevor said he would 'wash' the towels. I thought that a waste of time and soap. We all walked back to the checkpoint and needless to say there was no vehicle.

Johannes and I were left under guard some thirty metres from the main road and Trevor and Alpha went off to scrounge some cigarettes. After all the months of being hidden away we were now close to the road at a point in full view of the masses. Every vehicle, including buses and pedestrians, were stopped for examination of their passes. All passengers had to dismount and this was happening only thirty metres from where we were made to sit at the base of a telegraph pole. We were shouted at and abused and I realised that as Rhodesians we were being directly blamed for the air raids in which so many Frelimo soldiers had been killed. (Trevor told me later that some of the people were asking why we had not been killed!) We were there for some hours and I was desperately unhappy thinking enviously of Jon and Jim winging their way to Maputo and a better life. Johannes continued to say: "Not to worry. We will take off in a few hours." To my shame I remember getting very irritated with his false optimism and being rather short with him. The date was 22 December.

After dark a lorry arrived to take us back to the tent. On board was our evening meal and a large number of Frelimo soldiers who were to guard us that night. Because of the soft ground the lorry could not leave the road and we dismounted and walked the last kilometre or two. The meal turned out to be a dish of very wet saffron rice and a dish of pieces of fish floating in cooking oil. I decided to miss it. I suffered another sleepness night because of the mosquitoes. Just after dawn the next morning we rose and had a rub down with water from a large camp kettle. We made preparations for a possible hasty move when the call would come to proceed to the airfield for the eight o'clock take off. I was convinced the call would never come; and it did not. Later that day a Frelimo logistics commander came to tell us that a chartered aircraft had been ordered and that we would take off at 11 a.m. the following morning, Christmas eve. I did not believe him but Johannes did. We were hidden in the shade of the copse that day, both of us silent and miserable. Visualising Jon and Jim in Maputo having enjoyed a long hot bath, clad in new lice-free clothes, or maybe basking on the beach! Heavy rain was threatening and I asked for the holes in the tent roof to be repaired or covered and for a trench to be dug round the tent. However, nothing was done. At about ten that night the storm broke with a vengence and the rain poured through the holes in the tent. Both Johannes and I had placed our belongings clear of the holes but

Trevor and Alpha, who had moved into the tent when the rain began, had to plug the holes with their clothing. Some time during the night I woke to find that only the weight of my body was preventing my bed from floating off and that water was rushing past me on both sides. The plastic foam was saturated and I was lying in a pool of water. Ironically the ground near Trevor and Alpha was comparatively dry. I got up and after securing my bedding and clothing found a dry patch near the tent pole and spent the rest of the miserable night sitting there waiting for daylight. Johannes continued to lie in his pool of water.

The following morning was dull and overcast until about 11 a.m. and the heat was terrific. Everything was wet through and we certainly needed some blazing sun to help us through that day and the following night. Johannes continued to say: "Not to worry; we won't be here to-night"; I ignored him. How different for Jon and Jim snug in Maputo and probably enjoying a coffee or beer at this time. I again asked Trevor to organise the digging of a trench round the tent. He was well aware of the need but he could do nothing without a tool—the *badza* had gone—and the guard commander was not interested in obtaining one. Needless to say we did not take off that day and I realised that with Christmas Day on the morrow we were to remain in these desperate conditions until 27 December at the earliest and probably longer.

From our tent area we could see aircraft approaching and leaving, though we lost sight of them when they dropped below about 500 feet. According to Johannes every one that approached was 'ours' and he combed his beard in anticipation of a move. He was very proud of his beard and gave it much attention, pulling it down in front and curling the sides with his fingers. He often told me he intended to keep it after his release. My beard was thick and bushy and I regarded it as a nuisance. However, it did keep the mosquitoes from feeding in that particular area of my face. We were now without pills or tablets of any kind and I wondered how long it would be before we contracted malaria. We should be protected for another week or so by the tablets we had already taken.

Christmas Day was marked by the delivery, with the inedible meal of rice and floating fish, of a tin of condensed milk and a tin of mixed-fruit jam. We ate some of the rice mixed with jam and diluted the condensed milk to drink. As ever, once the tins were open the difficulty was to keep the creepy-crawlies out. We usually tried to get hold of plastic bags to tie over them or to stand the opened tins in water. This was not possible here for we had none of these bags and no containers for water. The guards were of no help. They were only getting one meal of *sadza* per day and fell on our abandoned food like hungry wolves. I thought that the cooks back at 'base' must think us more than satisfied with our meals for the food containers returned to them were almost licked clean. I was now beginning to feel the effects of starvation and the absence of the multivitamin tablets which had been generously supplied by medical orderly Africa. Once again it was a case of 'if only'. If only we had brought some of the reserves of food we had hoarded back in the guerrilla camp—the biscuits, at least, and perhaps some tins of sardines. "Leave it all behind," we had been told; we are going to Maputo, we had assumed.

Alpha and Trevor were not much better off than we were; they were surviving on some of the food we left and some of the *sadza* given them by the guards. As Trevor confided to me: "We are also prisoners." He was particularly upset, for after complaining to a Frelimo commander that he and Alpha had no blankets and that they were getting no food, he was brusquely asked: "What sort of a freedom-fighter are you, who cannot survive a few days without blankets and food?" However, they were free to come and go providing that one of them stayed with us. We certainly wanted one of them to stay for strangely enough they now appeared to us as friends and not the guards they had been; 'better the devil you know than the devil you don't' we reasoned.

On Christmas morning Alpha decided he would try to get some blankets and cigarettes for the two of them and some food and orange squash for Johannes and myself. He would walk to the nearest ZANLA headquarters in Tete and try to get transport to our old camp in the bush some forty or fifty kilometres away. Johannes and I did not hold out much hope of his succeeding and we suspected he had gone off to get a Christmas drink with his guerrilla pals. During that Christmas Day Johannes and I managed to get our blankets and clothes dry but the plastic foam never did dry out. Johannes promptly appropriated the dry mattress vacated by Alpha. We had no visitors or news of movement of planes during that day. Before dark, at about five p.m., the rain started again. The guard commander had been relieved and his successor was more humane and energetic. He quickly realised the necessity for a drain-trench and in the absence of a *badza* used a bayonet. As it was raining he insisted on digging a trench inside the tent and before dark had made a good job of it for the water being carried away. However, the ground inside the tent was soaked from the previous night and with a wet mattress beneath me I spent another miserable night. How long, O Lord, how long? Now no food, no sleep and nothing to smoke.

I was glad to see the dawn of Boxing Day and to be

able to stretch my legs a little. The rain stopped during the night and the sun was trying to break through the low clouds. Johannes was still sleeping. He seemed to have the good fortune to be able to sleep almost anywhere and to eat most foods except when he was feeling ill. There was some water in the camp kettle and I washed down my body and legs and then hung out the damp blankets and clothing. The humidity was such that even overnight my boots turned green. Another long day ahead; I determined to try to get some exercise by walking. A very short course round the tent was agreed to by the guard commander, and eventually I managed to extend it to about seventy paces. The jam was now spoilt and the tin of condensed milk was full of ants. However, Trevor managed to tear a piece of muslin from a mosquito net belonging to one of the guards and he strained the condensed milk through it to remove the ants. The day passed without further incident.

Sometime during the night Alpha returned from his mission which had been very successful: on the morning of Wednesday 27 December we woke to find lots of packets of biscuits, many tins of Russian sardines, some bottles of *Sumovit* orange squash, a packet of glucose sweets and a carton of 300 cigarettes, but no matches! He had also brought back four blankets and a transistor radio. A very stout effort indeed. Alpha was only in his twenties and at one time had been employed in the Country Club at Penhalonga. This was near my farm, but as I was not a member of the club, I had not seen him before my capture. After he had joined the guerrillas he had been wounded in north-eastern Rhodesia and had had his right arm shattered. On recovering he had been employed on logistic duties and this was now his job. He was a junior commander and because of his damaged arm carried a large automatic pistol instead of the usual

AK 47. The four of us enjoyed a breakfast of biscuits and sardines.

Some time during the morning when we were in the copse for shade I observed that some of our guards were entering the tent and helping themselves to biscuits. I went into the tent and packed them into a cardboard box brought by Alpha. As we were always being told in the memorable words of Mao Tse Tung, "Power comes from the barrel of a gun"; we had no power to stop them, but at least I could make it more difficult for them.

10

After half an hour after noon on 27 December, a Frelimo vehicle was driven up to us and we were delighted to see the spectacled security man sitting in front. Once again: "Move—Move now—The aircraft is waiting" was the order, followed by "You won't need that—Don't take that." However, we managed to take the sweets and two bottles of orange squash, and Trevor shared the cigarettes with me. The biscuits and the Russian sardines we left behind for, after all, we were going to Maputo which reputedly was a city flowing with milk and honey. We boarded the vehicle and Trevor and Alpha jumped in with us. The Frelimo guards waved to us and we moved off. Maputo here we come!

On arrival at the airfield we were left in the porch of the uncompleted building and I managed to obtain a match for my pipe from one of the labourers working on the building. The business of getting 'fire' for one's pipe or cigarette was always a problem; a box of matches seemed often worth its weight in gold. Soon we were ordered to proceed to the runway and rounding the corner of the building I was surpised to see that the only aircraft in sight was a small light plane, an Apache. At the gate we said farewell to Trevor. He was visibly moved at our departure; muttering "Perhaps we will meet in Zimbabwe" and "Remember me to Jon" he turned away. Alpha was not present for he had been sent off by the security man with a message to the ZANLA headquarters nearby. We all had a high regard for Trevor who, in spite of difficulties, had patiently dealt with our complaints and requests and had tried to cheer us up in our more depressed moments. He had been particularly fond of Jon. One day I would like to meet Trevor again in different circumstances.

After greeting the pilot and co-pilot, both Portuguese whites, we squeezed into the aircraft. There was not much room and my pillow sack and Johannes' greatcoat had to be stowed away in a locker. (There were seats for four passengers in addition to the two crew). Johannes and I were placed side by side at the back and the two security men occupied the two middle seats. We took off immediately. The clock on the instrument panel read 1315 hours I noted. What a wonderful feeling: at long last we were on our way to Maputo. Johannes and I looked smugly at each other and almost purred with delight.

Once we were airborne we were both fully occupied in trying to see something of Tete and the Zambezi River. It all looked so much better from the air. We had been flying for some time when we both observed that the sun, now in the western quarter, was on our left side and to the rear. This was odd because if we were flying to Maputo, almost due south, the sun should be on our right! Never mind—we would soon change course. However, we did not, and I tried to get a look at the compass on the instrument panel. I eventually managed to move in my seat and look at the instrument panel but could only see the bottom half of the compass. The needle was quivering on 190° and I was reassured for a time. However, there was the sun on my left and we must have been flying north-by-east. I stood up in my seat and then realised that I had seen the bottom of the needle and not the arrowed top which was hovering between 360° and 15°. So we *were* flying north by east. Johannes and I discussed this almost in whispers. Of course this was a blow; but at least we were leaving that ghastly tent and the dreadful climate of Tete. Perhaps another change of plan, and we were on our way to Dar Es Salaam in Tanzania? Below the aircraft we could see no signs of life, only a bright green swamp as far as the eye could see. The security men said nothing—not even to each other. Fatty appeared to be sleeping and his assistant Specs was busy killing flies. The two pilots talked and smoked all the time.

At about 3 p.m. the radio began to blare out in Portuguese and a little later we began to descend very gently. There was very thick cloud at low altitude and we did not break through it until about 1 500 feet. We had been flying at about 8 000 feet. The first place we saw was a huge prison camp with the usual guard towers. It appeared to be unoccupied. As we approached the airfield we could see a fairly large town nearby. The runway was a long one and the whole place seemed to be in good order. There were no large aircraft to be seen but many small planes such as the one were were in; there were also some very small helicopters. As we taxied in to the reception area we saw a large sign with the word 'Nampula' on it. I had never heard of the place before but Johannes said he had read of the place in some magazine or other. It was not far from the coast in the north-east of Mozambique. There was a rush to refuel the Apache and I thought we were to continue our flight. Fatty and the crew had left us but Specs remained in the aircraft as a guard. After some time he complained loudly that he could not understand the delay and that he was very hungry. Fatty returned and it appeared that we were to get off here but that something had gone wrong with the transport arrangements. After a time a Volkswagen

159

passenger vehicle drew up on the far side of the plane keeping the plane between us and a few interested spectators, most of whom appeared to be Portuguese pilots and air crews. We got into the vehicle which was very dilapidated and set off, destination unknown. (I had already dismissed all thoughts of Maputo but wondered why *we* shoud be so unlucky when Jon and Jim were probably living it up.) Fatty was in a private car being driven by a Frelimo soldier. As we were leaving the vicinity of the airport shouting broke out. It appeared that our transport had been found and this turned out to be a large army lorry which had been tucked away out of sight. We transferred to this vehicle and set off through the town. Strangely enough in this large vehicle we had only two guards in the back with us. However, they were very jumpy and looked as if they would relish the chance to shoot us. On one occasion I reached into my pocket to get some sweets for Johannes and myself and one of them had his AK 47 in my ribs in a flash. Evidently these Frelimo guards never took any chances.

As we drove through the town it was easy to see that the Portuguese had left many pleasant houses behind when they fled. Most of these houses appeared to be occupied by officials and officers and many had military guards outside. We passed a large barracks and what appeared to be a military prison before stopping to fill the tanks of the lorry with petrol. It looked as if we had a long drive ahead. We drove back through the town and then turned east. Once on the open road the driver travelled quite fast in spite of the size of his lorry and it was obvious he was in a hurry. I thought that the commander in the front of the vehicle wanted to reach our destination before dark because we only had two guards; not enough for his peace of mind. After about an hour and a half we turned off the main road which headed for the coast and passed through a small place named, I think, Maconta. Just beyond this village we could see a long low building within a white wall and surrounded by lights. I whispered to Johannes that we had reached a holiday camp but I recognised it as a prison. (Johannes told me later that he had not realised it was a prison.) We drove in through the gates and after dismounting we were searched. The contents of my pillow sack were also examined. They indicated that I could not retain the sack and so I hastily removed my towel, soap, toothpaste and toothbrush before they took it. We then heard voices from a nearby building and recognised them as those of Jim Black and Jon Kennerly, one of whom called out: "Welcome aboard."

Surprise, surprise. They had not gone to Maputo after all.

I remember asking them if they had enjoyed their Christmas on the beach and what they had done about the cold beers we had ordered! Their reply is unprintable. The door of their cell was not unlocked and we were appalled to see how small it was, how it stank, and that they had no bedding of any sort. Their Christmas had been no better than ours. Jim Black told me later that they were convinced that we had gone to Maputo and that they would not see us again.

Both Johannes and I expected to be put into a different cell from the others for this one was crowded with only the two of them in it. However, we were both thrust in and the door banged shut and locked. There was a light outside the cell which shone through the bars. Later that night we were each given a coir-filled palliasse, two blankets and a sheet together with a coir-filled pillow. We thought the sheet a joke in this filthy place but were glad of it later when the mosquitoes started to feed. The problem was to decide how we were going to fit four palliasses on the floor in such a small space. Jon had a problem for he was well over six feet tall. It was like doing a jigsaw puzzle. The floor space was 64 square feet (8ft × 8ft) and the four matresses totalled 60 square feet (4 × 6ft × 2½ft). There was no pacing this cell in the time-honoured way. The cell door opened inwards and so the spare 4 sq ft had to be behind the door. Even so we had to use this space for water mugs and boots and when the door was being opened we had to rush to clear away our mugs and boots. At the rear of the cell and inside it was the *latrina*. At one time there had been a half door on this but it had been removed. The *latrina* consisted of a pear-shaped lavatory basin close to the floor without any cover on it. The down pipe led into a sewage pipe under the floor which ran the whole length of the building, and if anyone used a latrine 'up-stream' as it were, it meant that their waste matter flowed through the pipe under the basin in our cell. There was no running water to any of the latrines and hundreds of fat yellow maggots made their way up the sewage pipe and emerged from the basin. They hatched out in the open cesspits beyond the prison wall. Johannes had a ragged shirt which he no longer wore and we stuffed that into the down pipe to keep the maggots at bay. However, when one wanted to use the *latrina* one had to remove the 'stopper' and then the maggots dropped off in hundreds. It was all rather nauseating.

When we finally got organised and spread our blankets I at first decided to sleep on the sheet for it was unbearably hot. However, I soon got under it because of the mosquitoes and eventually cocooned myself in it, head and all. Whoever supplied that sheet certainly knew about the mosquitoes and the following morning all the sheets were peppered with blood stains.

'Prison' is an emotive word and has different meanings for different people. I suppose that in Britain it means the loss of one's freedom and a stigma on one's family and close friends. However, I understand that there is exercise, radio and television, books and newspapers, bathing and washing facilities, letters in and letters out, visitors, employment of a sort, indoor games, and, most important, a definite date of release. After that there is assistance from the Prisoners' Aid Society. The prison we were in meant something entirely different. Four of us in a small cell designed for one; no reading matter, no exercise, no employment, no indoor games, no letters, no visitors, dreadful food, and not knowing for how long we were in. In addition we had no communication with our guards, who spoke only Portuguese.

I thought that we had been moved here as a sort of reprisal for the air raids on the Frelimo camps and that this prison had been chosen because it was almost as far as you can get from Maputo (with its International Red Cross and British Consul's offices) and remain in Mozambique. This place was almost ideal if you wished to keep prisoners incommunicado for a year or two. I also thought that if we stayed here long we would go mad. We continuously tried to improve our lot but it was a hopeless task with no common language. Jim Black spoke Swahili and one of the guards also had a smattering and so I asked Jim to explain that we must have some anti-malaria tablets or we would all be very ill. After what seemed hours of cross-talk the guard went away apparently understanding. Two days later the results were handed to us in the shape of a tin of insect-repellent spray! Later after Jon Kennerly got malaria and collapsed outside the cell in full view of the guards we were given two anti-malaria tablets each week. At this time Johannes was asking every day for his *muti* and showing off his scars to prove he must have it. He got no medicine at all yet he seemed none the worse for the lack of it. He even continued to eat well. We tried to learn some words of Portuguese but without a dictionary or phrase-book found it beyond us. If only one of the guards could speak English *and* Portuguese it might have been possible.

The commander of the guard was not a very pleasant fellow. He was quite young and not apparently senior (Frelimo wore no badges of rank). The guards addressed him as 'chief' and we talked of him as the 'little Corporal' which was about his limit. The guards were always more unpleasant when he was about. Among these guards we soon got to know the good, the bad and the indifferent. Although the prison we were in was staffed with civilian warders, we had nothing to do with them but were always guarded and attended by Frelimo soldiers. The other prisoners (all black, except for one Portuguese white and one coloured who shared the same cell) were never allowed to see us or speak to us. It was sometimes comical to see the frantic efforts taken to prevent us meeting or seeing each other. It was not easy in that small prison even though the black prisoners all went out to work and we were only allowed out for washing after they had left, and had to be in our cell before they returned in the evening. In fact, we were generally in our cell twenty three hours a day; we were allowed out for ten minutes to wash in the morning, twenty minutes in the late afternoon for a bath and sometimes for about half an hour for a meal in the prison yard. Our washing and bathing took place in this yard under a cold water stand-pipe.

For two or three days we had a most welcome break

when we were moved into a much larger cell whilst the door of our 'single' cell was strengthened and a new chain fitted. We were able to pace this fresh cell but alas it was not for long. There was no latrine there and so we continuously banged on the door to be allowed to go to a communal latrine in order to get some exercise and this was not popular with the guards as the yard had to be cleared before they let us out.

As can be imagined we were suffering mentally as well as physically under these conditions. Jon Kennerly and Jim Black were not on speaking terms and when Johannes and I had arrived at the prison we had noticed the tension between them. Apparently they had had a flaming row over the Christmas period. We were all under considerable strain and the small things began to irritate us and cause outbursts. I remember that a slanging match broke out one afternoon as to who would have a bath first (we were only allowed to go into the yard one at a time). Another afternoon Jon and Jim quarrelled violently over some minor matter. It was all rather childish and I am sure it was regretted later. Anyway Jon and Jim were persuaded to patch up their differences in the interest of us all but it was an uneasy peace. About this time I was having dreadful nightmares, some of which were about the maggots. I would wake in the night thinking they were swarming over us (after all they had less than a metre to cover from pedestal basin to bed) and I would have to go and look. In fact by morning some would have overcome the first stopper and were well on their way towards us. Others would come under the door from another latrine Sometimes I would wake and feel I would have to get up or I should scream, but there was nowhere to walk. One could only stand on the blanket and stretch one's arms heavenwards. My memory continued to play tricks and I wondered if I would ever completely recover. Although Johannes was as depressed as the rest of us he still had great faith in the power of the Lord and regularly prayed for all of us. Sometimes he would ask permission to pray aloud as he found that easier in English. He thought in Afrikaans.

We were getting two meals a day, at about noon and six p.m. One always knew what it would be for the meals followed a strict sequence. If one meal was *sadza* with a small quantity of fish, the next would be macaroni and fish and that was always followed by the rice and fish. All was soaked in cooking oil. Sometimes in the early morning we would get a dish of very sweet tea, almost white in colour from the tinned milk in it. There was a very large mango tree in the prison yard and we could hear the fruit dropping on the roof of the cell. We were always asking for these and sometimes we were given some. I had never liked mangoes before but certainly enjoyed them then, though unfortunately most of them were damaged by the fall. In the early days in the prison we were given some bananas. When we were allowed into the yard for a wash or a bath we immediately looked round for fallen mangoes and pounced on them. Invariably the guards had already done the same thing and those left were so badly bruised as to be inedible.

The washing of our sheets was a problem but we pestered until the 'chief' agreed that we could wash them in the yard. I had never washed a sheet in my life and found it most difficult under a cold water tap whilst trying to keep it off the ground. However, we welcomed the chance to be out of that cell for a time and took as long as possible over the task. I was obviously a duffer at the job for the guards were appalled at my efforts and one of them offered to help. They took them outside the prison wall to dry and always remembered to bring them in when it rained. However, mine never looked 'whiter than white'.

11

We were keen to find out some information about the white Portuguese prisoner. Through our 'spy hole' in the door we had observed him going out of the prison dressed in his best and without escort. At other times he was locked in his cell for days. He was a good-looking, well-built chap with a trimmed black beard, in his late twenties or early thirties. Sometimes the coloured man accompanied him. We were desperate to make contact with either the International Red Cross or the British Consul and Jim Black suggested we try and make use of the Portuguese prisoner who seemed to be able to leave the prison on occasion and could possibly post a letter to Maputo. At first we were worried that he might reveal to the prison authorities our attempt to contact him but eventually we agreed to write him a note. It should be of a simple, innocent character in order to test him out and safeguard us if it were discovered. Jim Black wrote a note asking if the Portuguese spoke any English, his name, and that of his companion. The note was thrown through the bars into his cell by Black when he was outside for a bath.

We received a reply, after dark, the following night (The Portuguese had no *latrina* in his cell and was allowed out at about eight p.m. to use a communal latrine before going to his bed). The reply was to the effect that he and his companion did not speak or read English to any extent, and gave their names. He also asked our names and other details. This prompt business-like reply pleased us although the lack of English was a disappointment. (Why is it we always expect people throughout the world to speak and understand English?) Still, he did have enough English to have read the note and to have understood it. Another innocuous note was written, giving our names and, to keep it simple, saying we were Rhodesian farmers, asking why they were in prison. Before we got a reply to this the Portuguese managed one night to toss a most welcome gift of a bag of locally-grown peanuts into our cell. All the prisoners except us seemed to get them regularly in their diet and we complained bitterly at this discrimination. The reply to our second note did not help us much for it was obvious that their English was too limited. However, we gathered that the Portuguese was in prison because of money trouble and the coloured man was in prison because of 'woman' trouble. We came to the conclusion that the Portuguese must have been in business in the local village and was allowed out to attend to his affairs. Like many others of the local prisoners he had his meals brought to the prison from his home. We all agreed that our third note should be the critical one asking the Portuguese if he was prepared to post a letter to Maputo for us. It was risky, for apart from the chance of his handing over the letter to Frelimo there might be postal censorship in Mozambique, and, further, we were expecting the Portuguese to pay the postage for we had no money. We decided to await a reply to his note before giving him the letter to Maputo. We never did get a reply to this note, for some hours after it was tossed into his cell things began to happen which made it unnecessary to write to Maputo.

Just after the noon meal we heard two vehicles draw up at the prison gates. This was so unusual that we all wanted to use the peephole at the door. We saw that there was a group of people at the gate amongst whom were the two Mozambique security officials, Fatty and Specs, and even more exciting, they were accompanied by Commander Darlington. He was a guerrilla on the staff of Robert Mugabe and was known to us all, particularly to Jon Kennerly who had been interrogated by him many months before. When we had been flown to this prison Darlington was meant to accompany us on 'liaison' duties but had been left behind, perhaps when the plan to fly us to Maputo had been changed and we had flown north instead. To see him again was a good omen for it meant that Robert Mugabe was still concerned with us and we were not destined to be left by Frelimo in this gaol and forgotten. They did not come to the cell; and after some time, they drove away. However, we thought that they would be back for probably they were waiting for darkness to fall before collecting us in order to conceal our movements. We were used to that.

Sure enough, just before dark they returned and we were told to pack, but to leave all bedding behind. We were told nothing of our new destination and although we questioned Darlington he would say nothing. We all got into the leading vehicle and I asked that we should collect the things that had been taken from us. This we did at the Frelimo headquarters in the village of Maconta. There was nothing missing. We then travelled to Nampula, with a Frelimo escort in a second vehicle; Fatty, Specs and Darlington were in our vehicle.

On arrival in Nampula we were given a meal of leftovers and then shown into a detention cell containing many double-bunk beds. This had obviously been hastily vacated for us as there were remains of a meal lying about. Each bunk had a plastic foam mattress impregnated with the sweat of the previous occupants and the smell from these and the lavatory was quite over-powering. There was plently of insect life and the walls of the cell were marked with red blotches where bugs had been squashed. However, we cared nothing for this, for we had left that awful prison and were on the move again. Perhaps this time to Maputo?

We were all awake early the next morning and ready to move at short notice. We were brought some sickly-looking tea and crusts of new bread which we enjoyed very much. At about eight o'clock we were collected by the trio and driven to the airfield. On the runway was on-ly one large aircraft, a brand-new machine painted green. We were told to board this using the lowered rear ramp. The plane was of Russian manufacture, built for parachute-dropping and for the transport of small vehicles, having securing clamps on the floor. The plane was so new that I conjectured that the crew must be fly-ing it with the instruction book open beside them. The crew of five were white and appeared to be Russians or East Germans. They were dressed in civilian clothes and did not speak to any of us. In front near the pilots' cabin were comfortable bucket seats but a partition and door separated this from the rear where the seating ran along each side of the body and was very austere. We were told to sit at the rear accompanied by Specs and Darlington and two men in civilian clothes who appeared to be security men. Fatty sat up front with the crew. We took off almost immediately and just afterwards Specs came to me and said: "We are going to Maputo."

"I suppose we are going into another prison," I remarked.

"No. That is finished. There, my government says, you are to be well looked after," he assured me, "but you will still be under guard."

"What is going to happen when we reach Maputo?"

"I do not know. You will be kept in a government house. The Foreign Office will look after you there."

Later he came to me and said: "The flight will take three hours and twenty minutes. Do you like the airplane?"

"It's certainly better than walking or going by lorry," I conceded, quite impressed by this effort at conversation; and added: "I notice that it wasn't made in Mozambique."

He smiled at this and said: "No. It's from our friends. We have lots of planes now."

We were very interested in the scenery and Specs pointed out the communal farming efforts which were being practised in Mozambique. We later followed the coastline but because of cloud saw nothing of Beira over which we flew.

When we landed at Maputo quite a crowd came up to the plane but there were no press men amongst them and it appeared that it was the aircraft itself which was the centre of interest for the airport workers. Fatty, Specs and Darlington faded away without a word. There were hundreds of soldiers to be seen and it seemed probable that most airfields in Mozambique had troops stationed on them. We were led over to the office of the airport manager where we settled, guarded by two armed Frelimo soldiers inside the office with numerous others being stationed in the passages and outside the building. I noticed an immediate change in the behaviour towards us for we were now being *asked* to do things and not *told* to do them, altogether a different atmosphere. We felt better already.

Just after we had settled in the office and had grabbed magazines to read the guard commander asked if we would like lunch. We all agreed that we would and were then led to a restaurant which appeared to be for the exclusive use of senior members of Frelimo and the airport staff. We had a good meal there (I think we all chose prawns or other sea-food with salad) and a soft drink to wash it down, followed by coffee. I had to restrain myself from putting some of the food in my pocket for the morrow. Then we went back to the office and the magazines. Later we returned to the restaurant for another meal and whilst there were told that transport was waiting for us. We could not understand this for it was still daylight! We split up getting into two cars with an escort in each, and set off into Maputo. The date was 31 January 1979.

I had never been to Lourenco Marques but Maputo, as it was now called, looked in good order to me with its large well-stocked shops. There were plenty of cars but mostly older, well-used models; more like the Salisbury vintage than Johannesburg. Later I was to notice that the pavements and roads were in need of maintenance. We were shown into a respectable detached suburban house in a tree-lined road not far from the centre of the town. At first we were quite lost, wandering around the lounge and dining room like children in a well-stocked toy shop. The previous occupants had left in a great hurry and appeared to have been Germans for there were dozens of *Stern* magazines and other evidence of their nationality. Later we were to find that the bedrooms had been very hastily vacated and that whoever they were, they had had living with them two or more children. The house was well and comfortably furnished with four bedrooms but it had only one bathroom, which was in great demand.

We each selected a bedroom. Apart from the mattresses there was no bedding but later we were each given a new bath towel, new sheets and a new blanket. In my room I had an enormous double bed, the first bed I had had to sleep in for six months! I did not sleep a wink, however, whether because of the bed or because of excitement I do not know; and Johannes Maartens confessed to me the next morning that he had not slept either and that he was going to sleep on the floor that night. The house had a staff of sorts who all appeared to be plain-clothes security policemen. We were told we could have what we liked to eat and that some drink was being obtained for us. That evening we were joined by an official of the Mozambique Foreign Office who said we should call him John. He was a coloured man, very tall and good-looking and altogether a charming man. Perhaps I. was unduly impressed for between us we drank a lot of whisky. He said that it was his pleasant task to look after us for a few days and that he hoped to have some good news for us on the morrow. After some time he asked if we would like a tour of the town and seafront in a car and we jumped at the chance. A second car was organised to contain an escort.

It was then about nine p.m. We had a most enjoyable tour and looked longingly at the many hotels and night spots on the sea front. However, we certainly were not dressed for those places as we were still wearing our 'bush' clothes. Perhaps another time.

The next morning John came to the house and told us we were being handed over to Amnesty International for release. This release could take place in the next two or three days! Meanwhile we were to be taken to a Frelimo building in the town for photographs, and a conference. We still wore our beards and Johannes was anxious to have a photograph of himself showing his beard. The photographs were taken and John joined us for them. He promised that we would be given copies before we left for Maputo but I never did get those copies. Anyway, perhaps we looked too awful. When we got into the conference room John sat with us. Presently we were joined by Commanders Emerson and Darlington who were both on the staff of Robert Mugabe. However, we were not too happy when Emerson said we would be released in a month or two! He addressed this remark to Johannes Maartens who for some unknown reason accepted and agreed with this. John, the Mozambique Foreign Office official, obviously did not and before the remaining three of us could voice our objections we were ushered out to another room under guard. That left John, Emerson and Darlington to sort it out in the conference room. I complained bitterly to Johannes that he might be happy about another month or two but I certainly was not, particularly after we had been promised release within two or three days. He had no right to agree for the four of us. He surprised me by replying that he had not meant what he had said. However, the issue was settled by the Mozambique Foreign Office official. Emerson, accompanied by Darlington, stalked grimly past the open door of the room in which we were waiting, and John joined us to say that his remarks that morning about release still stood. Our release had been arranged with Amnesty International and would not be altered. What did we want to do now? Both Jim Black and I wanted to have our beards off and Johannes reluctantly agreed to have his off also. Jon Kennerly was more than in need of a haircut for it was below his shoulders. We were driven to a rather superior salon and the other customers were asked to leave. Guards stood at the door while we were dealt with by the Portuguese hairdressers. After their operations I thought that Johannes looked ten years younger, Black looked more haggard and I looked about ten years older for the hairdresser had almost shaved my head as well as removing the beard. However, there was no putting it back.

We were warned that after lunch we would be taken

back to the conference room. When we did go back we waited for a time and were surprised when the President of ZANU, Robert G. Mugabe, walked in. With him were Vice-President Simon V. Muzenda* and Secretary General Edgar Z. Tekere**, also Justin Nyoka, Commanders Emerson, Darlington and others.

The President was dressed, as before, in a well cut safari-suit with long-sleeved jacket and long trousers. After they were all seated he said: "You are being released into the care of Amnesty International, tomorrow, on humanitarian grounds. There will be no conditions attached to your release. You can go where you like and say what you like but if you return to Zimbabwe you may again become casualties."

To his question, put to each of us in turn, "Where do you want to go?" we all replied: "Rhodesia." He threw up his arms in a gesture of resignation.

"You will be handed over to the Amnesty International officials," he continued, "after a press conference at the Polana Hotel tomorrow afternoon at 2 p.m." As many reporters and correspondents from all over the world were gathered in Maputo at this time attending a conference of 'nonaligned states', our release was timed to fit in with the conclusion of this conference in order to gain maximum publicity for Mozambique and Samora Machel.

The President then asked us each in turn about the state of our health and whether we had any problems. When he came to me, he said with a smile: "How's your stomach?"

That was fine now I told him; but in answer to his

* First Deputy Prime Minister of Zimbabwe.
** The first Minister of Manpower Planning and Development in Robert Mugabe's government.

question about problems, asked: "Can I have my medals returned before I leave Maputo?"

He looked nonplussed and asked me to explain what I meant. I told him that they had been taken by his men and that I had been promised their return.

He frowned. "I know nothing of this." He turned rather stiffly to Commander Emerson and said with some exasperation: "What do you know of this? They should not have been taken. You must make enquiries and find them."

Turning again to me, he said with restored affability: "Anyway, you can surely get another set. The British are good at that sort of thing."

Our entire interview had been marked by a pleasant friendliness and there was no hint of the disagreement between Emerson and the Mozambique F.O. official that morning about the date of our release.

After Commander Emerson had informed us that he would take us shopping the next morning to get some decent clothes they all left. Obviously we were not to got to the press conference in rags although in fact we were now better dressed than we had been for six months. The period in prison, with our almost complete inactivity, had enabled us to protect our clothing.

After the departure of Robert Mugabe and his entourage we were told to stay seated in the conference room where later we were joined by the two Amnesty International officials who were to be responsible for us after our release. They were Dick Oosting, a Dutchman, and Malcolm Smart, an Englishman. They were efficient, friendly and generous. I cannot over-praise their zeal and enthusiasm to make the next two days most pleasant for us. Perhaps in the euphoria and excitement we did not thank them properly or enough, but I will never forget their efforts on our behalf. Why the International Red Cross did not supervise our handover was never clear to me but certainly Amnesty International did the job very well although I gathered it was not their usual function. Dick and Malcolm explained the situation and the time table: it had been suggested to them that we should be handed over at Komatipoort, on the Mozambique—South African border north west of Maputo and then proceed by road to Johannesburg. Did that suit us? It suited Johannes who had a brother in White River not far from Komatipoort but the remaining three of us, remembering the cramped journeys in vehicles over the past five months, asked whether we could fly from Maputo to Johannesburg. Johannes fell in with this and it was agreed upon. We were also told that after release we could move into the Polana Hotel until we boarded an aircraft. As we were comfortable in the government house, however, we elected to continue sleeping there but decided to spend the day-time in the hotel where we could telephone our relatives. This was Thursday 1 February. That night John took us on a tour of the town and after parking the cars, and accompanied by a plain-clothes escort, we walked round the shops. They all seemed well stocked and I noticed a John Orr store with good displays.

The following morning Emerson and Darlington called for us and we did some shopping at the expense of ZANU. We bought shirts and pants and later we were given socks, shoes and a safari suit each, and more underpants. However, except for the shoes, the articles bought for us did not fit and this proved a difficulty, for the next day, Saturday, was to be a public holiday to commemorate the death of the first black President of Mozambique and all shops would be closed. They were also closed on the Sunday. Emerson would not be beaten by this: he managed to get hold of the shopkeeper who had supplied the safari suits and persuaded him to open his store for us on the Sunday morning. We changed our suits but the underpants and socks, which were too small, had come from another shop and could not be changed.

12

Dick and Malcolm had warned us that the press conference would be intimidating and that we must control our tempers. It was to be held in the grounds of the Polana Hotel at 2.30 p.m. on Friday 2 February—that afternoon in fact. We were duly escorted there arriving at about 2.20 p.m. 'Intimidating' was an understatement. There seemed to be hundreds of correspondents, male and female, near the swimming pool of the hotel. Their array of equipment—cameras, microphones and tape-recorders—defies description. We were kept under guard, close to the hotel building, and although several correspondents tried to anticipate the opening they were kept at bay. The conference was late in starting but eventually we four were shown to chairs to the right of the VIPs who were seated immediately behind a battery of microphones. At this point many of the correspondents came up to congratulate us asking us to have a drink with them later, and we posed for lots of photographs.

There were many speeches by Mozambique and ZANU officials including Robert Mugabe and Secretary General of ZANU Edgar Tekere. The gist of them was that we were being released unconditionally on humanitarian grounds and that we were free to go anywhere and to say anything we chose. We would be invited to talk to the Press about our experiences but could refuse if we wished. We all elected to answer questions from the floor and I went to the microphones first. I cannot remember the questions and answers now but I do remember committing a *faux pas* which caused a lot of laughter. One of the first things I had been told after my capture was that I must never refer to my captors as terrorists. They were guerrillas. I had managed to remember this except for a few times when I had been reprimanded for speaking of terrorists and of Rhodesia. However, on this most important occasion I forgot, and in front of the assembled Press spoke of terrorists when referring to my captors. After the laughter had subsided I felt my shirt pulled from behind. Sitting directly behind me was Robert Mugabe and with a smile he said to me: "Be careful, or you will find yourself back with us."

After we had all spoken we were formally handed over to Dick Oosting and Malcolm Smart. *We were free.* After that I must have resembled a 'dream walking' for I never knew what to do or where to go next. That evening we had a wonderful dinner in the hotel as guests of Dick and Malcolm. I ordered prawns and received such a large quantity I was unable to finish them. Again from force of habit I almost put the unconsumed portion in my pocket and regretted not having a 'doggy bag'. We were so much in demand from the press representatives that it was a problem to remain sober; but of course with the Press we were expected to sing for our supper. I remember one American correspondent asking me if I would like to do a lecture tour in the States—accompanied by the 'little woman' of course. It was all rather overpowering. That night we were late back to our government house for we had difficulty in rounding up everybody, particularly young Jon Kennerly who was in great demand. Fortunately he did not take alcoholic drinks but even so looked pretty 'high' on the soft variety.

The next day, Saturday, was a holiday and so shopping was out of the question. In any case we had no money, although we thought it high time someone provided us with some escudos. After breakfast at the hotel (I do not know who paid for that; and did not enquire) we were taken to the British Embassy for documentation. Jim Black and I suspected that our passports had been stolen when our houses had been robbed after our capture. Jon Kennerly had never had a British passport and Johannes knew that his passport had been safe in his house in Rusape. In spite of it being a public holiday, and therefore most of the Embassy staff being absent, two British officials worked like beavers to get us temporary passports in one day. Because of the holiday there was a problem over photographs. However, somebody knew sombody who had a Polaroid camera and attempts were made to contact him. The subject of payment cropped up and the three of us who had filled in forms were asked how the British authorities were going to recover the equivalent of eleven pounds sterling from each of us. (How typically British!) At this time the British Government was giving millions of pounds in sterling as aid to Mozambique and, after our dreadful experiences, we were being asked to refund the cost of a passport. But the books had to balance. This comment is not meant as a criticism of the Embassy staff, who preformed wonders that day; they had regulations to follow. We all promised to refund the money in Rhodesian dollars to the British representative in Salisbury, if there was such a person, and we then returned to the hotel. Later that afternoon the owner of the Polaroid camera arrived to take our photograph. Of course the resultant pictures were too large but skilful cutting produced the regulation size, head and shoulders. I remember hoping that my photographs was not a good likeness: that barber had done nothing for me and I thought I must have looked better with my beard. That evening we received the completed passports.

Dick and Malcolm told me that Robert Mugabe was having a reception that evening and that they had been invited. I asked if I could use the telephone in their room, whilst they were out, to ring Jennifer's brother in Pretoria and ascertain her whereabouts. I also wished to telephone my daughter Elizabeth in Johannesburg. They readily agreed. I got through to Pretoria very quickly and spoke to Jennifer's brother, David Cowan. He told me that she had vacated our farm the day I had been taken and that she had been living with Pat and Strace Stroud in Penhalonga near Umtali. She was now flying from Salisbury to Johannesburg and he and his wife Ulla, and daughters Lydia and Dorothy, were about to leave to meet her. They would all be at Jan Smuts airport to meet me the following evening. This was wonderful news for I had had no word of or from Jennifer since bidding her farewell on the 1 August the previous year. I was very pleased to hear that she had been staying with the Strouds, our neighbours at Odzani. They were a very level-headed, kindly couple who would have looked after her well. They must also have vacated their farm and moved to Penhalonga for they had been on holiday in South Africa when I had been abducted! I also got through quite quickly to Northcliff, Johannesburg, and spoke to my grand-daughter Jane. It was a joy to talk to Jane again and I was pleased to hear that while I had been away she had graduated. Later that evening I rang Pretoria again and spoke to Jennifer, and this was the highlight of a wonderful day.

Returning to the hotel I met Dick and Malcolm.

They had just returned from drinks with Robert Mugabe and had been given four thousand escudos for the four of us, one thousand each. This was a kind thought: but alas we could not spend it. Our meals and drinks were being paid for by all and sundry, and all shops were closed the following day, Sunday. Someone said we should be able to change it into South African rands at the airport before take-off, the next day, but this turned out to be false. However, we did manage to buy a large tin of cashew nuts each from a small shop near the airport which exhausted the meagre stock of the store. Malcolm told me that he had raised the question of the payment for the passports with Robert Mugabe and had been assured that ZANU would pay and would also pay our fares as far as Salisbury. One of the correspondents who overheard this laughed and said he did not know how they were going to do this for as far as he knew ZANU was already in the red. I thought this unlikely with all the vast sums being allocated to them, particularly by the Scandinavian countries.

The next day, Sunday, was take-off day and we were to leave for the airport at five p.m. In the morning we were collected by Emerson and Darlington and taken to change our ill-fitting safari suits. Each of us was also given a cheap suitcase for our belongings. These suitcases were a bad buy, for Jon Kennerly packed and locked his and later found he could not unlock it; mine burst open before I reached Pretoria. After a long wait in the VIP lounge of the Maputo airport we took off at 8.35 p.m. We were seen off by many of the senior members of the ZANU Central Committee and by officials of the Mozambique Government and the British Embassy. Whilst waiting I had a long conversation with Didymus Ne Mutasa*, the ZANU Deputy Secretary for Finance.

* Didymus Ne Mutasa became speaker of the new Zimbabwe House of Assembly.

He was familiar with the area in which my farm was situated and knew of all my friends and neighbours. As I had found with other senior members of ZANU he made no attempt to talk politics—instead we both spoke of the wonderful beauty spots in the area of Mutasa. He told me of many I had not seen; and would not see until the war was over. He was a quietly spoken, educated man, and I enjoyed our conversation. He appeared to be homesick for Rhodesia. During our long wait for take-off a senior member of the ZANU High Command asked if any of us was likely to be in Salisbury for long. Jim Black said he thought he might be there for a time and he was then asked if he would pass on a message of goodwill to a retired prison warder (who was named). This man had been their guard when some of the ZANU officials had been in detention in Rhodesia and they had appreciated his sympathetic and kind attitude to them. They wanted him to know they had not forgotten him and wished him well in his retirement.

13

We touched down at Jan Smuts airport at 9.30 p.m. and from then on all was confusion. Another aircraft was standing by to take us to Salisbury but Jennifer had planned for us both to spend a week in Pretoria. I was all for this as I felt quite ill and was passing blood in my urine. I had noticed this two days before at the Polana Hotel but had not mentioned it for fear I might be left behind in a Mozambique hospital. We were all quickly taken into the VIP lounge and the Rhodesian Foreign Affairs official agreed, rather grudgingly I thought, to my spending a week in Pretoria before returning to Salisbury. The Press, in large numbers, were outside the lounge, desperately keen to interview us. However, the officials did not want this, because a TV and press gathering had been organised in Salisbury.

Of my relatives only Elizabeth and Jennifer were allowed into the lounge. Jon Kennerly was met by his parents and Johannes was being smothered by his large family. Jim Black had no relatives in Rhodesia or South Africa and after shaking hands with me he set off for the Salisbury aircraft. Johannes looked very ill and had staggered off the plane like a drunken man but we knew that he was not ill: he was suffering from having taken some sedatives and then foolishly drinking some whisky afterwards. Before he had entered the aircraft he had been looking very fit and happy. Johannes' wife, Jean, came up to me and shook hands. I had not met her before but after my capture she had kept in touch with Jennifer and they had been a comfort to each other, keeping each other informed of any news they had received. They had worked in concert for our release and had travelled together to Jan Smuts airport from Salisbury. Jennifer was very fond of her. (I would like here to thank the many relatives and friends who continuously made efforts to secure my release.)

Jennifer had made many trips by air to Pretoria to contact the British and South African authorities, and also wrote a personal letter to the President of Mozambique, Samora Machel. Much later she received a reply, dated 24 January 1979. I was shown a copy of this letter by a Mozambique Foreign Office official on the day of my release. My friend, Air Commodore D. F. Hyland-Smith, wrote a moving letter to the British Foreign Secretary asking him to secure my release. A former business colleague in England, Richard Johnston, pressed Amnesty International to do something on my behalf and many others contacted the International Red Cross. There is no doubt in my mind that this continuous pressure on the Mozambique Government was responsible for their insistence on our release. Later I learnt that the British and South African Governments had also put pressure on the Mozambique Government to release us. Since there were no diplomatic relations between Salisbury and Mozambique, no help was forthcoming from that direction. In the confusion I left the lounge without saying goodbye to Johannes and Jon which I regretted. Once outside the lounge Jennifer and I were almost swamped by the Press and instead of stopping and answering a few questions we tried to outstrip them. This was unsatisfactory from everyone's point of view. Once clear of the reporters I met my son-in-law, Alec, and my grandchildren, Jane, Simon and Victoria. Also with them was Jennifer's brother David, his wife, Ulla, and their children, Lydia and Dorothy. I was back home. That night Jennifer and I talked the whole night through and I learned many things. Jennifer was full of gratitude for the sympathy and practical help she had received from our friends. Jim and Myra Valintine had taken her into their house for the first month after my capture and later she had moved in with Pat and Strace Stroud in Penhalonga after their return from South Africa and was living with them up to the time of my release. Friends in need are friends indeed and I was very grateful for the way they had all supported her in her time of trial.

As we talked, I discovered the official report of my capture was completely wrong. Jennifer had been taken to Penhalonga Police Station and shown on a map the route along which the police claimed I had been taken into Mozambique on the day of my capture; she had been told that tracker dogs had followed my tracks to the border where I had got into a vehicle. What nonsense! I had been held in a guerrilla camp inside Rhodesia for four days and had crossed the border far to the south of the point they had indicated to her. There was certainly no vehicle involved. I wished there had been. For many weeks after my return I was to hear incorrect reports of my capture from individuals who had heard it from somebody else, and so on, until the source of the false information was obscure. The reports had me going directly east from my point of capture instead of along my actual route, north and then west to a guerrilla camp in Rhodesia. This was either rumour at its worst or a deliberate effort to frustrate any follow-up. One report which angered me was to the effect that I had *gone willingly* with the guerrillas and that they were carrying my clothes (which indeed they had stolen) for me. This was a bit hard after all I had suffered after my capture: somebody had been the willing or unwilling tool of the guerrillas and was spreading false information. I remembered then that the commander of the guerrillas who had captured me had confidently told me there would be no follow-up; which made the course of events the more mystifying.

Some of the press reports of my abduction were wrong in every particular and confirmed my long-held opinion that you cannot believe all that you read in the papers! One newspaper cutting which Jennifer had kept reported that we had been held in Maputo for six months! It seemed to me that the police had obtained their information from blacks in the area who had previously been briefed by the guerrillas on what to say in order to confuse the authorities.

Europeans, presumably unwittingly, had helped in this by accepting what their labourers had told them without question. However, although I was angered at the time by the absence of 'follow-up forces', there is now no doubt in my mind that if my captors had met the Security Forces I would have been killed. That was the usual practice and no doubt accounts for several abductees who have disappeared without trace. Another surprising thing I learned from Jennifer was that my medals had been returned to her in October via Penhalonga police station. Apparently they had been found on the clothing of a guerrilla who had been killed in the Security Forces' attack on the Chimoio camp in September. Truth is certainly stranger than fiction and I would have had difficulty in believing that if I had read it in a book. The medals and miniatures were complete except for missing oak leaves, but in a very dirty state as one would expect.

Jennifer also showed me three letters, taken down

by a woman previously unknown to either of us, and purporting to come from a spirit with the name of Theodora. The woman is Mrs Nella Southerden and apparently she has quite a reputation locally as a medium. However, we had not heard of her or met her before my capture. I have the letters in my possession now and I was astonished at the accuracy of their contents, particularly of the first one dated 17 August 1978 and timed 3 p.m. Although these letters were written by Mrs Southerden at the dictation of the spirit Theodora the writing is not like her own. To prove this she had endorsed the letters in her usual style. However, she assured Jennifer that she has been in communication with the spirit Theodora for a long time and we have now had confirmation from other people in her area who have had evidence of her powers in the past. Both Jennifer and I have always been sceptical of this sort of think but there is no denying the evidence of the letters. Mrs Southerden did not know Jennifer and did not originally intend to give her the first letter but was persuaded to do so. This was sometime in September. After this she got two more letters from Theodora, dated 13 October 1978 (2.10 p.m.) and 4 January 1979 (4 p.m.). Below are the contents of the letter dated 17 August 1978, seventeen days after my capture and whilst I was still being held in the bush near Chimoio camp in Mozambique. I had had no messages from Rhodesia for the whole period of my captivity nor did I get any message out of Mozambique before December 1978. The letter said:

Dear Nella,
You have been asking for news from the gentleman who was abducted we see him in his camp it is very hot and very dirty so many barbarians surround him he has to do things against his will he is shrewd

and he is doing all he can to avoid the worst but he is under stress he walked far but he was quite used to it from experience he got very thirsty he is eating porridge and bad food now but he knows hardships he will survive he is trying to get a message to his devoted lady this lady must not worry she will see him again he is telling her she must have courage he is alive he wants her to go to a more safe place he worries for her they will have food together again in some little home together and laugh too much he will come home to her in some while too many people are helping him also mostly God our Heavenly Father he has got sore on his feet from walking all savages make him listen but he will come back he is alright he only wants his devoted lady to stay in safe place we hear his thoughts he is much perplexed for lady must send letter to him tell him she is safe he will be too happy soon he will come back he is very courageous and laugh at bad smells too bad sanitation savages too unhygienic Love yours in Spirit
Theodora

The letter printed above is as it was written without correction to punctuation. I have made many inquiries into the phenomenon and given it much thought and am now convinced that it is genuine. I find it uncanny. It has been suggested that the contents of this letter could be termed 'an intelligent appreciation of the situation' or in plain language a 'reasonable guess'. However, it must be remembered that at this time, 17 August, many local people thought that I was already dead.

14

The following morning it was agreed that priority must be given to medical checks and dental treatment for my broken teeth. David was very well known in Pretoria and was able to get me immediate appointments with doctors and dentists. The blood in the urine necessitated my entering a nursing home for twenty four hours but eventually within the week I was pronounced fit to travel. I certainly was most grateful to Ulla and David for that week for I felt a different man compared with my state when I got off the aircraft from Maputo. We travelled to Salisbury without fuss and touched down at about 8 p.m. We noticed that during the flight all windows had to be blacked out—a precaution adopted since the shooting down of the Viscount. Jennifer had parked the car at the airport and had booked a room at the Jameson Hotel. We were surprised to be given VIP treatment and a small reception had been laid on for us by Mr Allan of the Rhodesian Foreign Affairs Department. During this we were joined by our good friends Alan and Florence Constable.

The following day, Sunday, we spent visiting friends in the Salisbury area. Monday was to be a heavy day with official visits to various government offices and a debriefing. It had already been made clear to me that I had been naughty in not returning to Salisbury with the others for I had missed the press and TV conference and the debriefing. I pointed out that I had felt ill at Jan

Smuts but I was then told that I was to have had a thorough medical check at the Andrew Fleming Hospital in Salisbury. I wondered why they had not told Jennifer all this before we ex-prisoners had landed at Jan Smuts. The debriefing was a bore and seemed to go on and on. I do not only mean that it went on for a long time but also that when I thought it had finished there were always others who wanted to debrief me the next day. I got the impression that they were just very interested people, not the professionals. The most professional were the South Africans, who were high ranking: they asked the most penetrating questions. They appeared to know a good deal about ZANLA. Some of the Rhodesians adopted an attitude which seemed to suggest they knew it all already but they had to go through with the formalities. Perhaps they were right, for they had already debriefed Kennerly, Black and Maartens. However, as an ex-military man I thought they asked the wrong questions. Never once was I asked to show the location of the camp in Rhodesia at which I had been kept prisoner for four days. Another thing I found irritating was that the Rhodesian debriefers simply could not believe or did not want to believe any good about the guerrillas. They were all terrorists and beyond the pale. This was immature thinking and Johannes Maartens was the proof of care and kindness on the part of the guerrillas. There had been good and bad as in any body of men. Some of the officers and officials questioning me said they could not understand how we could be released alive and apparently well. We really should have been killed. There was sometimes a veiled suggestion that we must have promised something in return for our freedom. They simply did not know or realise that ZANLA had been instructed to release us by the Mozambique Government and had unwillingly complied.

This suspicious attitude of some Rhodesians reminds me of an incident in 1945 after the end of the Second World War, when I was responsible for a sector of the newly created border between West and East Germany. My area was the boundary between Kreis Lauenburg (British Zone) and Kreis Mecklenburg (Russian Zone). The Russians opposite me were Mongolian infantry, very crude and barbaric in their behaviour. They were front-line fighting troops. Raping and looting were hourly occurrences. They lived off the land and their rations were allocated to them 'on the hoof' from the nearest farmer's stock.

I spent six months on this duty, and every day had its disquieting events. One grim incident occurred when I escorted a young Russian officer to a border post for handing over to the commander of the Russian troops opposite my sector. At this time there were a number of these Russian ex-prisoners-of-war wandering round the British Zone and our orders were that they were to be rounded up and handed over to the commanders over the 'line'. My opposite number was a difficult man to deal with. He was quite senior and had a reputation of being over-fond of the local women and drink. He would, or could, only speak Russian and I used a Polish officer (ex-P.O.W. of the Germans) who was attached to my unit as an interpreter. The Russian commander made it clear he was not interested in taking the young Russian officer. He said: "There are no good Russians in the west. He must be a deserter." After a lot of talking and shouting he moved off with the ex-prisoner under guard walking in front of him. After thirty or forty paces I could hear the two officers arguing. The younger Russian was made to stand on the grass verge and was then shot by a burst of sub-machine-gun fire from one of the escorts. Accompanied by the Pole I crossed into the Russian Zone and asked for an explanation. I received a lot of shouted Russian in reply and the Pole looked quite shocked. When he was asked to translate he would only say: "The Russian commander says that it is none of your business. He says the man they have shot is a deserter." No inquiries, no reference to records. A harsh demonstration of the fact that at this time the Russians were very suspicious of any of their countrymen who had had contact with the western way of life and did not want them to return to Russia.

I had given much thought to the reasons for my being abducted rather than killed. We had tied down many guerrillas as guards as they were very nervous of escape attempts or efforts by the Security Forces to rescue us. In addition they did go to some trouble to vary our diet once they were convinced we could not stomach *sadza*. In my own case I was told that they suspected I was connected with the Security Forces, for reasons mentioned earlier and was important enough to have some value as a hostage. In September we had been informed that attempts had been made to effect an exchange of the four of us for some of the ZANU leaders in the hands of the Salisbury government; later we were informed that Salisbury would not co-operate in this. (This was understandable for if this exchange procedure had been started no one in Rhodesia would have been secure against abduction). On another occasion I was told by a commander that the abductions were carried out to prove that the Security Forces could not give protection to individual whites and to 'encourage' farmers to leave their lands. This was probably the main reason, for the abductions helped to spread terror, if only locally.

Jennifer had already told me that our farm was now occupied by the army and had been converted into a company-defended locality. Much against her wishes I decided I must visit the place. I wanted to get the story of my capture from Kenneth, my 'boss boy'. I expected him to tell lies to cover himself and could understand his reasons for doing so for no doubt he had been threatened with death or worse if he did not lie. After being in Penhalonga for some days I went to the farm (some twenty miles away) and I was appalled at what I found. The place was a shambles, with all the buildings occupied and the surrounds of the house converted into bunkers, M.G. positions and the like. I was now without home or employment.

Kenneth greeted me warmly and with tears in his eyes. He had always seemed to be able to cry very easily. Perhaps this had helped when he had pleaded with the guerrillas not to kill me when they captured me.

As I had expected his version of my abduction did not agree with the facts as I already knew them, but he stuck to the story he had told the police and army personnel. He was a kindly man, somewhat sensitive and very nervous, and I certainly was not going to try and exact revenge from him.

He had been told what to say by the guerrillas and had said it, for if he had not he would not be alive today. These black Rhodesians working for the whites in the rural areas were 'between the devil and the deep blue sea'. They had to be very slippery and fast-thinking to keep alive or out of prison.

He asked: "Are you well, master? How is Madam?" This was his usual greeting when we met. He went on quickly: "I asked them not to kill you. We all did. I told them that you are a good man. I told them you brought back my family from behind the wire." He appeared to be very frightened and I realised that he did not know how much I knew of his part in my capture.

"Yes, they told me," I replied, "but why did you tell

the police they only came at seven that morning? Why did you not tell them that I was taken in the direction of Bradley's farm, and not towards Lake Alexander?"

He replied: "I did not know you were taken through Bradley's farm. We were all taken into the laundry and made to lie on the floor. We were told to keep quiet or we would be killed. They locked the door and we could not see anything." (In fact the laundry building had no lock on the door and later they had let themselves out.)

I again asked: "Why did you tell the police that they were taking me for broadcasting?" (This apparently was where the broadcasting story had originated.)

He shifted uncomfortably, looking irresolutely to the side and downwards as he answered: "We were told to say that. We only knew what they told us. When we were in the laundry we heard the guns and we were very frightened."

"Why are you frightened now?" I asked, for I felt that he must by now be reassured that *I* had no vendetta against him. "You are here with the army," I pressed.

"I am frightened of the soldiers."

"Have the soldiers beaten you?"

"No, but I want to leave. I have told Madam."

It seemed to me that not only was he worried about the possible action I might take against him but also frightened that the guerrillas would label him a 'sell-out' (traitor), as to all appearances he was now working for the army. He was obviously desperately nervous at Odzani, but had stayed out of loyalty to me. He was our only remaining labourer for Jennifer had dismissed the others when the army had moved in. Moreover, he had proved himself a valuable and reliable employee in the days before my abduction. Since he was not assured of employment elsewhere, I could not feel that his departure would be an advantage to either of us.

197

"Now look, Kenneth," I began, "I want you to stay. Thank you for asking the guerrillas not to kill me. I will look after you," I continued, "and when I find a house in Umtali I will come for you and your family. The police will not take you away." So I persuaded him to stay, hoping that I was not condemning him to death by so doing. When we later moved into a house in Umtali, our property at Odzani still being occupied by the Security Forces, I moved Kenneth and his family to Umtali to work for me there.

We had lost that season's fruit and vegetable crop which had been a blow, and altogether we had lost heavily financially. Jennifer would have to continue her job until we could get some compensation for our stolen goods. That would have to be our top priority. However, I knew the insurance company would not accept liability for enemy action.

During my captivity I had only wished for my release and reunion with those I loved. I would be more than satisfied with that, I had told myself; I had no desire for money and possessions. However, after 'the nine days' wonder' one had to face reality and find somewhere to eat and live, and obtain the means to pay for it. Still, my awareness of the good things of life had been sharpened and it was almost as if I had been born again. I again enjoyed a sundowner and good tobacco in my pipe.

There had been many occasions when I had expected to die and now I was very much alive. The most simple things that were usually taken for granted like flowers, trees, scents, walking, the love and devotion of dogs, good food, clean sheets, clean clothes, hot water for baths and so on, meant more to me than ever before. I suppose that it is all summed up in one word: freedom. Certainly I had no desire to 'collect' anything again and would only replace items that had a practical use. So we rented a house in Umtali and set about replacing some of our stolen goods and clothing.

About a fortnight after my return to Umtali I had a very odd experience. I was standing outside Checkers store in Main Street when I was approached by a tall black man dressed in blue overalls. He came up to me with a surprised look on his face and said: "How are you? What are you doing here?"

I did not recognise him. I replied: "I am well. Who are you?" He suddenly seemed at a loss and looked confused. I then asked him: "Where have we met?"

He replied: "It must have been at Inyanga."

I told him that I knew Inyanga but did not remember meeting him. He looked apprehensive and I thereupon said jocularly: "It must have been in Mozambique." At that he took to his heels and ran away. It seemed to me that he had seen me as a prisoner but had forgotten where and when.

The situation in Rhodesia was still very dangerous and uncertain but we decided to stay and see how things worked out. Both Jennifer and I loved Rhodesia and, in spite of our unpleasant experiences, were not convinced we would be happier in South Africa or the U.K. Both these countries seemed to be going through trying times and we did not relish the idea of jumping out of the frying pan into the fire.

At the time Ian Smith, supported by the Rhodesian Front, was desperately trying to protect the future of the white minority and he disdained to take the easy way out by leaving the political arena after majority rule. However, it had long since seemed to me that once Mozambique had closed the port of Beira to Rhodesia and offered a haven to guerrillas raiding into Rhodesia we were fighting a war we could not win. Man for man,

Rhodesian Security Forces were far superior to their opponents; but there simply were not enough of them and they did not have 'the support of the masses'. The Rhodesian blacks in the rural areas could not be protected from the intimidation, threats and reprisals of the guerrillas and thus they were lost to the Security Forces. The other important consideration was that the guerrillas had widespread support from other black states and countries in Eastern Europe. Their weapons and equipment were almost expendable items. Surely this was the time—1976—when the Rhodesian leaders should have seen the writing on the wall and compromised whilst they still had some control, and before Kissinger and Owen became so involved? In spite of high-level statements to the contrary, time did not appear to be on the side of Rhodesia; and as it grew stronger the Patriotic Front was increasing its price. Ian Smith's problem was that there were always so many black claimants to the Rhodesian power seats with whom to deal. In my opinion a strong dedicated leader *was* emerging and that was Robert Mugabe. It was too late to compromise with him. He had much support from both within Rhodesia and without and from what I had seen of the members of ZANU/ZANLA they were prepared to fight to the end, regardless of the cost. They seemed very confident of victory and there was talk in Mozambique of the political members of ZANU being trained for government administration. Some of the ZANLA commanders, I recall, had nothing but criticism for Joshua Nkomo's ZIPRA, claiming that they were doing very little in the war and were merely kept in being as Nkomo's 'private army'. Certainly there was much hostility between the rank-and-file members of ZIPRA and ZANLA and reports of their fighting each other were frequent. It was often conjectured that if the war between the Security Forces and the guerrillas ended in a victory for the Patriotic Front a civil war would break out between the two armies forming that uneasy alliance. Other blacks would no doubt take sides.

As for me, everyone I met after my return to Rhodesia said: "You were very lucky." I suppose I was lucky to have returned alive and in one piece. However, I thought I was unlucky to have gone through that experience at all: certainly I had suffered physically, mentally and financially. I was always meeting and hearing of individuals who were doing very well out of the war, and I met many people who would be worse off if and when the war was over. Some of the elderly gentlemen who interviewed me in Salisbury appeared to be completely out of touch with the situation prevailing in the more remote rural areas.

I believed that the longer the war went on the more difficult it would be to secure a peaceful future for the whites in Rhodesia. The black population was suffering extreme hardship and misery. They appeared to be blaming the white population for this state of affairs and might be slow to forgive. Certainly they would demand more equality of opportunity and an immediate improvement in their standard of living from whoever formed the government.

However, I had always found the blacks in Rhodesia to be gifted with commonsense and a marked sense of humour. They have a proverb: "He who forgives ends the quarrel." And for me any 'quarrel' was over. We would stay in Rhodesia. I had confidence that peace and prosperity was not an unreasonable hope if only the political leaders could agree.

POSTSCRIPT

The foregoing was completed in April 1979, within two months of my return from Mozambique. The following months were both frustrating and irritating. It was incredible to me how naive most of the whites in Rhodesia were. How could they not understand why the countries outside Rhodesia (with the possible exception of South Africa) refused to accept the March Agreement between Bishop Muzorewa, Ian Smith and the Reverend Sithole and the results of the following election? And yet it must have been obvious that the whole charade was a waste of time and money: the blacks had not attained majority rule although they had been given the vote. The whites had the right of veto in the government. Even more important, the nationalists leading the guerrillas were not included in the election process. The war that the Rhodesian Security Forces could never win would continue until the country was ruined.

In spite of this, the popularity of Ian Smith and the Rhodesian Front seemed to continue and few whites would accept criticism of them. It seemed to me that after years of censorship and a controlled Press and radio most people had ceased to think for themselves and were thoroughly brainwashed. It should have been obvious to all thoughtful people that we were going to finish with an agreement that would be more demanding of the whites than one which had been possible years before; and before the loss of thousands of lives and the immense suffering of blacks and whites alike.

Before the March 3 Agreement the Rhodesian Front Party had made a complete about-turn with its policy towards majority rule but I cannot recall any R.F. Member of Parliament resigning his seat on a question of conscience. It seems that politicians can call the tune but do not feel obliged to pay the piper. I sometimes wished that some of them had been abducted.

After the March 3 Agreement many black leaders claimed that they could 'stop the war' and prevail upon the guerrillas to return to peaceful pursuits. However, this was not the case and the war continued. It appeared that the guerrillas were loyal to Robert Mugabe and Joshua Nkomo and the fighting would continue until those two called a halt. Umtali experienced more mortar and machine-gun attacks and a new horror was inflicted on its people with the placing of bombs in shops during daylight hours. Fortunately a change of government in Great Britain brought about the Lancaster House Agreement and, after the long years of conflict, a 'ceasefire' at last.

There was some talk of a scorched-earth policy and mass emigration in the event of a Mugabe victory at the elections but his moderate speeches and behaviour after his overwhelming success had the whites reluctantly agreeing that perhaps he, Mugabe, was not as bad as he had been painted and the general decision appeared to be that 'we must wait and see.'

I was full of admiration for the part played by the British in the negotiations and subsequent supervision of the ceasefire and election, but many whites were convinced that the 'Brits' had intended all along that Mugabe should win. I disagreed with this view. There was no disputing that intimidation and threats had affected the voting to some degree but it appears that ZANU(PF) would have won without it. Before the election I made a point of asking every black I was acquainted with, whom he wanted to win and without exception they replied: "Mugabe". They were not concerned with marxism or communism but only wanted the fighting to stop and in their opinion only Mugabe could bring that about. Some whites were saying, fearfully: "You mark my words. There will be many changes!" I replied: "But that was what the war was all about."

One of the odd things about the election was that most of the whites were unable to exercise their votes. Of the twenty seats allocated to whites fourteen of the Rhodesian Front members were unopposed and no elections were necessary. This was resented by many but illustrates the complete control that the Rhodesian Front exercised over the white citizens of Zimbabwe.

After the election a remarkable change took place in the security situation. Many more people travelled outside the towns, most without weapons of any sort, renewing acquaintance with the wonderful views of the Vumba and Inyanga. An estate agent friend told me that there had been an upsurge of property values and that some properties that had been on the market had been withdrawn. Rumour was rife as is not unusual at such time: the Rhodesian Light Infantry was to be disbanded overnight; every member of the Selous Scouts had received a threat against his life; no person would be allowed to own more than one house; petrol was coming off ration but doubling in price; there were queues of emigrants at Beit Bridge—and so on. However, one was also hearing of and meeting families returning from the U.K. and South Africa to live in Zimbabwe. Apparently they were disillusioned about the way of life and cost of living in those countries.

After the initial shock of the election results it was generally agreed that perhaps it was all for the best. If Mugabe's victory had not been so absolute there would have been enmity and rivalry between the political leaders. More intimidation and fighting would have occurred between the rival factions and the whites would have become targets for all. Surely now Zimbabwe could become a truly multi-racial country with peace and prosperity for everyone—an example to the whole of Africa. Certainly, with the co-operation and aid now promised, only wise and moderate leadership was required. What kind of national leader would Robert Mugabe become?